How to pay off your mortgage in 6 to 8 years:

Wealth habits of the rich that will save you thousands

By

Joe Correa

COPYRIGHT

This publication is designed to provide accurate and authoritative information in regard to the subject matter covered. The examples and information in this book may not be accurate and should be reviewed by your financial adviser. If financial or legal advice or assistance is needed, consult with a qualified attorney, accountant, financial planner, or bank representative. This book is considered a guide and should not replace consulting with a mortgage professional. The author, publisher, and all representatives are not responsible for any action you may take financially. For tax purposes consult with an accountant to review your tax options depending on your particular situation. No part of this book shall be copied for any reason at all. No part of this book may be reproduced or transmitted in any form or manner.

ACKNOWLEDGEMENTS

This book is dedicated to all the people in the world that owe money and want to get out of debt. I hope you use the concepts in this book to eliminate debt and start living financially free. Most people never realize they are living financial slavery until it's too late. It is my wish to end financial slavery in the world by making people wiser in the ways of money by giving them the tools to build a better future.

How to pay off your mortgage in 6 to 8 years:

Wealth habits of the rich that will save you thousands

By

Joe Correa

INTRODUCTION

How to pay off your mortgage in 6 to 8 years: Wealth habits of the rich that will save you thousands

By Joe Correa

Want to pay off your mortgage and be out of debt?

This book has the solution. It's full of valuable ideas and examples that others have used to eliminate their mortgage debt in just a few years. You will learn how to minimize expenses and plan your pay off strategy in an organized and practical manner.

What do banks offer as a solution?

Most banks only give you one option which is basically to send your payment every month for the next 30 years. Yes, you will have paid off your mortgage by then but there's a better way. A faster way and easier way that requires simply planning for what needs to be done.

Do you have a 30 year mortgage?

Do you have credit card debt?

Do you make insurance and property tax payments?

If you answered "yes" to any of these questions, you can seriously lower your mortgage debt and the time it takes you to pay it off. If you answered "no", there's still other options that are explained in detail.

Most books give you general ideas as to what you can do to eliminate your mortgage debt but this book shows you how it's done with real examples and solutions.

You will see how payments amortize, how much interest goes towards payments, and how much interest you will pay over the life of the loan when presented with different solutions.

Why is paying off your mortgage important?

Having a 30 year mortgage can be a blessing and a headache at the same time. Most people finance their first home while in their 30's which means they will finish paying off their mortgage in their 60's if not later. When you finally pay it off, you will have eliminated one of your largest monthly payments and you can now start saving a lot more than before. Guess what? You are around retirement age or coming close to it so what will happen to your income? For some, it will remain the same. For others, it will decrease slightly. And for many, it will disappear and you will have to live off your retirement savings for however long they last. Having less expenses sooner than later will equate to more savings for years to come and having less payments to make will reduce the financial burden when you have retired.

Taking proactive steps towards paying off your mortgage sooner will change your life. It will allow you to free up time to do what you really want to do and work less.

Pay off your mortgage and start living the life you have always wanted! Go on vacation, spend time with loved ones, or start a new business.

ABOUT THE AUTHOR

For many years I have helped people to finance their homes or to lower their payments. I have worked for different banks, lenders, and a large investment advisory firm. I started as a college math professor at Miami-Dade Community College teaching all math subjects I was asked to teach at age 23, which was kind of awkward for many of my students as many of them were around my age or older but my ability to teach others and to master math helped me make difficult subjects easy to understand. That's why my classes became larger and larger. I was approached by Union Planters Bank which is now Regions Bank, one of the largest banks in the country, and worked for them as a Financial Sales Representative at one of their branches. This was an important learning stage for me that allowed me to see the value in helping others. On a daily basis, I was required to open the bank doors, open the bank vault, open personal and business bank accounts, complete home equity lines of credit and home equity loans, and many other tasks. I especially enjoyed closing home equity loans and wanted to learn more so I got my mortgage license and went to work for a mortgage company on a commission basis.

Everybody was busy. There was so much work and so many banks eager to lend. A year later I started my own mortgage business and soon transitioned to a correspondent lender, which later became one of the top

100 in the state of Florida. I was able to help hundreds of people to buy a home, refinance to lower payments, and to take cash out to pay off debts or reinvest. When the economy slowed down and banks slowed down lending I decided to focus on helping investors by becoming an investment adviser. I got my series 67 license and started my own investment advisory business. Most investors had lost trust in the economy and did not want to reinvest so I decided to help others by educating them. I hope this book reaches as many people as possible and helps shape a new future for many that might feel stranded on their own without a solution.

CONTENTS

PREFACE

In general, having a 30 year mortgage is better than having a lease since you will eventually own something when it's paid off. It's a start but owning a home without a mortgage or a lease is the end goal.

Paying off your mortgage sooner will have these positive effects on your life:

- It will allow you to save more money.
- It will reduce the amount of financial stress you have.
- Make your life simpler and easier to manage.
- It will free up time to do other things.
- Save you a lot of money in interest.
- Be able to spend more time with family and less working.
- It will free up cash you could be investing in other projects.

Making it your goal to pay off your mortgage sooner should be on the top of your "to do" list because of all the benefits it brings. Learn to play the game using newer and better tools that are at your disposal if you read this book and find out what they are and start putting them into action.

Remember to always write down your goals and read them every day to make them reality. This is a common habit ultra-successful people have and is simple to accomplish. Paying off your mortgage and all other debts should be your primary focus since it opens your life to more opportunities.

What type of life do you want for you and your family?

Having debt and having the responsibility of making payments every month can be very difficult. Knowing that your job is vital to your ability to make payments each and every month is stressful and makes you feel like you're forced to work instead of working because you actually enjoy what you're doing. For that reason, figuring out a solution to this problem is what we are going to do in the chapters ahead.

Why do you pay your mortgage?

Everyone makes mortgage payments with the hope of paying it off one day and eventually owning your home free and clear but it often feels like a never ending road. At the beginning of the life of a 30 year mortgage, for example, your monthly payments go mostly towards paying interest and only a small portion goes to principal. During the first few year years you will notice the loan balance does not go down very much.

Who owns your home?

You own your home but many times you will feel like your mortgage owns you. If you sell your home the bank gets paid and you receive the equity that is left in the home but if you don't sell, you need to have a plan to pay off the mortgage sooner than 30 years to save on interest payments.

The power of ownership

Owning your home makes you feel in control. It makes you feel like you're on the right path to a bright financial future. This is wonderful but it will only be bright if you plan your future. Making mortgage payments for 30 year is not a bad thing but you could be better off by paying it off sooner and this should be your end goal when it come to your home finances.

Rent vs own

Renting a home can be something you have a choice over or sometimes you're forced to because you can't afford a home or because you don't qualify for a mortgage. In either case, finding a solution to this problem is important because the sooner you buy a home, the sooner you can pay it off and lower your household expenses significantly. If you have less payments, you can save more money and retire sooner or invest in another home or in your business. There's so much you can do with the extra cash when you've paid off your mortgage.

A 30 year mortgage is a big commitment

Making mortgage payments for 30 years is a big commitment and for that reason it's always better to know what options you have to pay it off sooner and reduce the financial burden it can cause on your present and future lifestyle.

Mortgage insurance

Mortgage insurance will not be used in the examples in this book since there are ways of eliminating mortgage insurance by either putting 20% down payment or having 20% in equity when refinancing or by getting lender paid mortgage insurance. Most banks will allow one or more of these options. Always find a way to eliminate mortgage insurance from your mortgage payments.

CHAPTER 1

The reality of paying a mortgage for 30 years

"Debt is the slavery of the free"

Publilius Syrus

I should start by saying I love numbers. Numbers are accurate and honest. They tell the truth of what's really going on. For that reason, we will go over different options of which some will apply to you and some will not but it will still be valuable information that will improve your financial life. In the end, improving your financial life should improve your life as a whole by allowing you to have less stress and more free time to do what you love. Use the vocabulary section at the end of this book in case some terms are not clear but it should all be pretty much self-explanatory.

In April of 2007, right when the entire economy was going down fast, we all learned an important lesson. Real estate does not always go up and if you buy at the wrong time you could end up being negative on the equity side of things. Meaning, you could buy a home at $300,000 and years later it ends up being worth only $200,000 depending on the real estate market and where you live as some areas have sharper ups and downs. This makes you realize that real estate can be speculative investing and that figuring out when to buy can make all the difference in the world. Real estate goes through a cycle just like all other financial markets. When the demand for houses is high and homes are in short supply (Too many buyers and not enough sellers), prices go up and then when there is too much supply and not enough demand prices go down (Too many sellers and not enough buyers).

What does this all mean?

Well, it tells you that you need to focus on what you do have control over instead of worrying on whether you are buying a home during the wrong end of a real estate cycle.

What do you have control over?

You can control the terms at which you finance your home based on the options that are available at the time. You can also control how fast you pay off your mortgage and how soon you own your home free and clear. Having no debt on your home gives you a lot of flexibility and reduces the financial strain of having monthly mortgage payments.

So, you can't control the economy or the housing market but you can control how you manage your finances.

This book will go into detail as to how to best manage your finances so that you can pay off your mortgage sooner than the bank proposed 30 year time frame most people get.

For simplification purposes we will assume certain numbers when we do our calculations even though they might not be specific to your case, it will give you an idea of what you could be doing with what you have. Decimals have been rounded up for simplification purposes.

Standard information that will be repeated

For home purchases we will assume a $300,000 purchase price. For refinances we will assume a value of $350,000. For a 30 year mortgage we will assume an interest rate of 4.5% and the same for 15 year mortgages. Normally, rates for 15 year mortgages are lower than 30 year mortgages but to keep the numbers constant we will use the same rate for both.

What is a 30 year mortgage and why do people get a 30 year mortgage instead of a term with less years?

A 30 year mortgage is a promise you make to the bank in the form of a lien which is placed on the house until it is paid off or until you sell the property. **Most people get a 30 year mortgage because it offers the lowest monthly payment** which for most people makes the most sense in the short term but we will learn that there are better ways of going about paying off a mortgage.

A 30 year mortgage looks like this:

You buy a home for $300,000.

You get financing in the form of a 95% mortgage which would be: $285,000.

Which means you made a down payment of 5% which is $15,000.

Your monthly mortgage payments look like this with an interest rate of 4.5%:

30 year monthly mortgage payments: $1,444

15 year monthly mortgage payments: $2,180

10 year monthly mortgage payments: $2,954

For simplicity sake we will not go over adjustable mortgages which have an adjustable rate after a specific period of time such as 5, 7, or 10 years.

What do you see?

The 30 year payment is the lowest and the 10 year payment is the highest. The 10 year payment is roughly twice as much as the 30 year payment but the mortgage is being paid off in one third of the time which is a big benefit if you can afford it.

Now let's consider the interest being paid off over the years for a 30 year mortgage since that is what we are focusing on in this chapter.

We are now going to look at a 30 year amortization schedule which is basically how much of your mortgage debt is paid off each year.

Total monthly mortgage payments are $1,444 and your total debt at the end of each year is approximately:

Assuming you start making payments in April.

Year 1: $280,402

Year 2: $275,593

Year 3: $270,564

Year 4: $265,303

Year 5: $259,800

Year 6: $254,045

Year 7: $248, 025

Year 8: $241,729

Year 9: $235,143

Year 10: $228,255 **(After 10 years 33% of your mortgage should have gone down but only approximately 20% has** gone down which means more of your monthly payments have gone towards interest, not principal)

Year 11: $221,050

Year 12: $213,515

Year 13: $205,633

Year 14: $197,389

Year 15: $188,767 **(After 15 years 50% of your mortgage should have gone down but only approximately 33% has gone down which means more of your monthly payments have gone towards interest, not principal)**

Year 16: $179,748

Year 17: $170,315

Year 18: $160,449

Year 30: $0 **(Mortgage is paid off.)**

Total payments made after 30 years which is the same as 360 months would be $519,858.

The total interest payments would be $519,858 - $285,000 = $234,858!!!

I skipped years 19 - 29 because this book is about focusing on paying off your mortgage sooner not towards the last years and this can be done through smarter actions and good planning.

This is an eye-opener for many people as they don't realize what they got themselves into. If you're planning to sell your home within the first 6 - 8 years then this is not relevant information but still very useful in case you have a friend or family member who is planning on keeping their home for a longer time period.

As you can see after 10 years you still owe 80% of the mortgage and after 15 years you still owe 66% of the mortgage. This is the passive approach to paying off a mortgage. This is the way the bank proposes you pay off your mortgage so that they can collect 30 years' worth of mortgage interest payments and by having you pay the majority of interest in the first years, they minimize their risk. This is simply a business transaction and you agree to go through with it because it allows you to buy a home you would otherwise not qualify for. You can take a better and quicker approach to paying off your mortgage. You will see the first approach on the next chapter.

How much interest was paid?

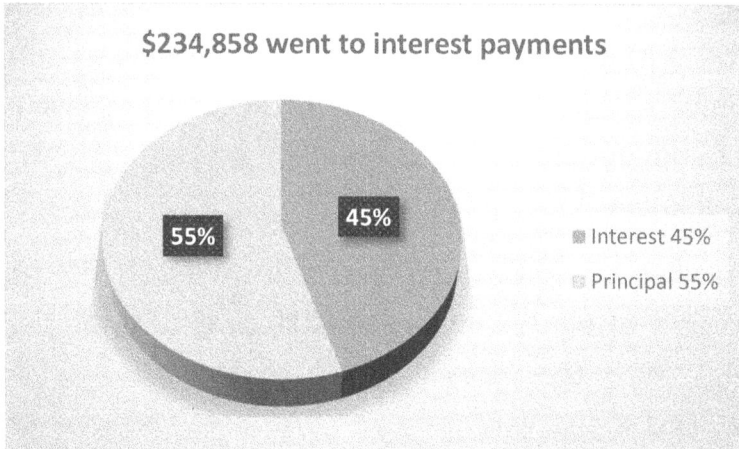

$234,858 went to interest payments

45%

55%

Interest 45%

Principal 55%

By paying off your mortgage in 30 years and made no additional payments you would have paid **$234,858 in interest which means 45% of your payments went towards interest** and 55% towards principal. What would you do with $234,858 if you could use it for another purpose? What if you could learn a way to save a large portion of this amount? Most people don't know what steps to take to reduce the interest they pay on their mortgage but better options exist.

Let's get started finding better solutions to pay down your mortgage at a faster rate!

KEY POINTS TO REMEMBER

1. You will always pay the most interest when you get a 30 year mortgage versus a shorter term.

2. The monthly mortgage payments are almost always the lowest on a 30 year mortgage but you also pay mostly interest at the beginning of the 30 year term.

3. After 10 years of mortgage payments on a 30 year mortgage term, you have only paid down 20% of the mortgage debt.

4. After 15 years of mortgage payments on a 30 year mortgage, you have only paid down about 33% of the mortgage debt.

CHAPTER 2

How Jack and Samantha paid off their mortgage in 15 years

"Debt is the worst poverty"

Thomas Fuller

I receive a call from Susan, my loan processor: "Joe, we have a customer who wants a 15 year mortgage".

"That's great. Please schedule an appointment so that we can sit down in person and go over there specific situation." I replied.

"They want to know what rate we offer on a 15 year fixed mortgage." She answers.

"Tell them I can't quote them a specific interest rate until I have more information. I need to know how much of a down payment they are putting down, if it's a purchase or refinance, what their credit scores are, their income, etc. This way we can be accurate with the information we provide them." I answered.

This is how the morning started but in the afternoon they were able to stop by my office and explain their situation.

How it worked out

Jack and Samantha wanted to keep their mortgage payments low but also wanted to pay off their mortgage sooner than 30 years and pay less interest over the term of the loan. They decided that they wanted to have a 15 year mortgage since they could still afford to make the mortgage payments even though they were higher than a 30 year mortgage.

Jack and Samantha's 15 year mortgage looked like this:

They bought a home for $300,000.

They got financing in the amount of $285,000 which means they financed 95% of the home's value.

They gave a down payment of 5% which is $15,000.

Their 15 year monthly mortgage payments with an interest rate of 4.5% was $2,180.

Now let's consider the interest being paid off over the years for a 15 year mortgage since that is what Jack and Samantha wanted.

We are now going to look at the amortization schedule which is basically how much of the mortgage debt is paid off each year.

Total monthly mortgage payments are $2,180 and their total debt at the end of each year is approximately:

Assuming they start making payments in April.

Year 1: $271,384

Year 2: $257,142

Year 3: $242,246

Year 4: $226,665

Year 5: $210,369

Year 6: $193,324

Year 7: $175,496

Year 8: $156,849

Year 9: $137,346

Year 10: $116,946

Year 11: $95,610

Year 12: $73,293

Year 13: $49,951

Year 14: $25,536

Year 15: $0 **(Mortgage is paid off in full.)**

The total interest payments after 15 years or 180 payments are:

$392,442 (total payments made) - $285,000 (loan amount) = **$107,442.**

Total Interest paid for a 30 year mortgage is $234,859 – $107,442 (total interest payments made after 15 years). By paying their mortgage in 15 years instead of 30 years they saved **$127,417 in interest payments over the life of the loan.**

What a difference it made to make payments for 15 years instead of 30 years. Jack and Samantha saved on interest over the life of the loan and finished paying off their mortgage in half the time so they have 15 more years to enjoy life with lower monthly payments than someone who has a 30 year mortgage. Hurray!

How much interest was paid over 15 years?

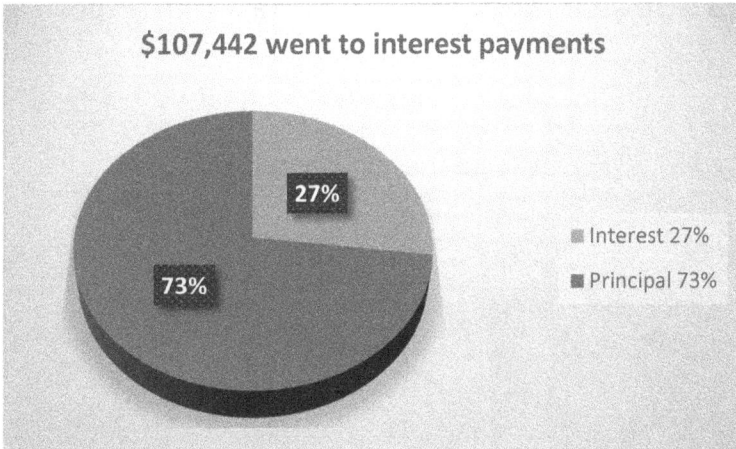

$107,442 went to interest payments

27%

73%

Interest 27%

Principal 73%

By paying off your mortgage in 15 years you would have paid $107,442 in interest which means only 27% of your payments went towards interest and 73% towards principal. This is half the time it takes you to pay off a 30 year mortgage and you end up saving $127,417 in interest payments.

Having a 15 year mortgage does mean you will have higher monthly mortgage payments but in the end it saves you a lot more money which you can now save for retirement instead.

How much did you save in interest payments if you compared a 30 year mortgage to a 15 year mortgage?

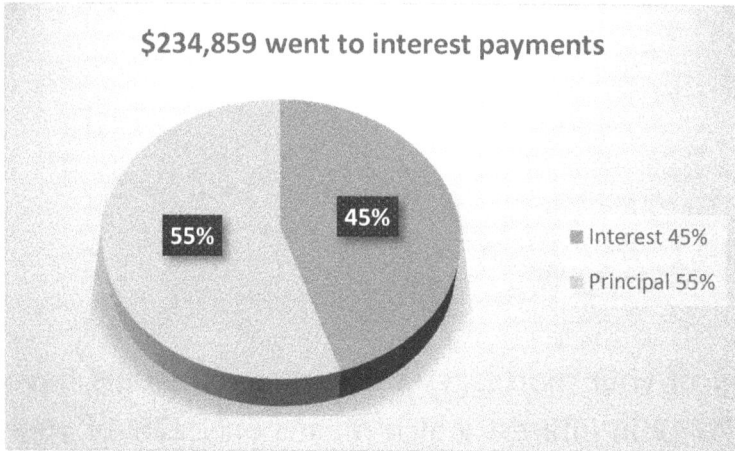

$234,859 went to interest payments

55%   45%

■ Interest 45%

■ Principal 55%

By paying off your mortgage in 30 years you would have paid **$234,859 in interest which equates to 45% of your payments going towards interest** and 55% towards principal. On a 15 year mortgage, you would have paid only 27% interest payments and 73% in principal payments.

45% - 27% = 18%

You would make 18% more interest payments with a 30 year mortgage than with a 15 year mortgage. This 18% equates to $127,417 you paid extra for having a 30 year mortgage!

KEY POINTS TO REMEMBER

1. Even though the monthly mortgage payments will be higher, you will pay down your mortgage debt in half the years when you get a 15 year mortgage versus a 30 year mortgage.

2. You will save a substantial amount of money in interest payments when you get a 15 year mortgage instead of a 30 year mortgage.

3. Most of the time, interest rates are lower on 15 year mortgages versus 30 year mortgages so you will save on interest in that sense as well.

4. Obtaining a 15 year mortgage is a smart financial decision when you can afford the payments.

CHAPTER 3

How Jill and Tom paid off their mortgage in 13 years and 5 months using bi-weekly payments

"Creditors have better memories than debtors."

Benjamin Franklin

A lovely couple came to my office one day inquiring about a mortgage. They mentioned they wanted to pay off their mortgage sooner than the usual 30 year term as they were working hard to retire within the next 30 years and didn't want to have mortgage payments once they retired.

I asked them: "Have you ever heard of a 15 year mortgage?"

Tom answered: "Yes, of course."

"If you can afford the payments, this would be a good option to consider, but the choice is yours once I show you the difference in payments." I replied.

Jill asked: "Is there something else we can do to reduce the amount of time it takes to pay off the loan?"

"Yes, you can make additional payments every year or use a bi-weekly payment method which would allow you to finish paying off your mortgage faster." I answered.

Jill asked: "How would that work out."

"Well, you basically end up making 26 half mortgage payments annually, which would end up being 13 total monthly mortgage payments" I answered.

Jill and Tom: "Great, that's what we want!"

How it worked out

Jill and Tom decided to have a 15 year mortgage and wanted to make bi-weekly payments so that they would end up making an extra payment at the end of each year towards their mortgage. Bi-weekly payments are basically payments every two weeks instead of once a month. For people who receive salary payments every two weeks, it makes perfect sense. It also works well for most people who can afford to make the payments.

Jill and Tom's 15 year mortgage looks like this:

They bought a house for $300,000.

They got financing in the form of a 95% mortgage: $285,000.

Which means they put a down payment of 5% which is $15,000.

Their monthly mortgage payments with a 4.5% rate looked like this:

Their 15 year monthly mortgage payments are: $2,180 but decided to make bi-weekly payments so their payments every two weeks are about $1,090 which will equate to 13 monthly payments annually.

Now, let's consider the interest being paid off over the years for a 15 year mortgage since that is what Jill and Tom have.

We are now going to look at the amortization schedule which is basically how much of your mortgage debt is paid off each year.

Based on bi-weekly mortgage payments of $1,090, their total debt at the end of each year is approximately:

Assuming they start making payments in April.

Year 1: $269,204

Year 2: $252,682

Year 3: $235,401

Year 4: $217,326

Year 5: $198,420

Year 6: $178,647

Year 7: $157,964

Year 8: $136,332

Year 9: $113,706

Year 10: $90,041

Year 11: $65,288

Year 12: $39,398

Year 13: $12,319

Year 13 (plus 5 more monthly payments): $0 **(Mortgage is paid off in full.)**

Assuming there is no prepayment penalty for paying off the mortgage before the loan matures.

How much interest was paid using bi-weekly payments?

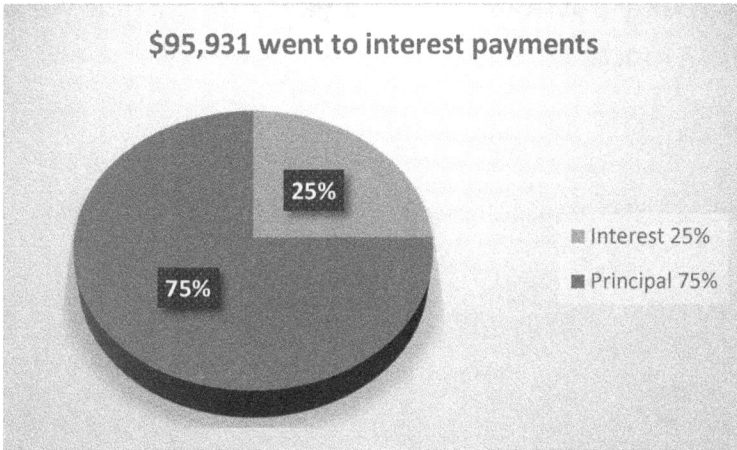

$95,931 went to interest payments

25%

75%

Interest 25%
Principal 75%

By using bi-weekly payments on a 15 year mortgage you will end up paying off your mortgage in 13 years and 5.

You would have paid $95,931 in interest which means only 25% of your payments went towards interest and 75% towards principal.

If you chose not to make bi-weekly payments you would end up paying 2% more interest payments over the life of the loan.

How much would you save in interest payments if you made bi-weekly payments on a 15 year mortgage instead of a 30 year mortgage?

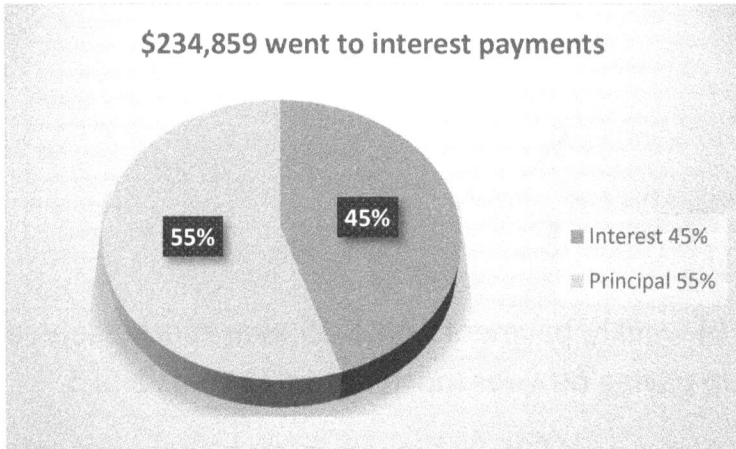

$234,859 went to interest payments

45%

55%

- Interest 45%
- Principal 55%

By paying off your mortgage in 30 years and did not make bi-weekly payments you would have paid **$234,859 in interest which means 45% of your payments went towards interest** and 55% towards principal. This is 20% more than having a 15 year mortgage with bi-weekly mortgage payments.

45% - 25% = 20% more interest paid at the end of the life of the loan when you have a 30 year mortgage and did not make bi-weekly payments.

KEY POINTS TO REMEMBER

1. Bi-weekly payments require that you make two half mortgage payments every two weeks.

2. Making bi-weekly mortgage payments will result in an additional mortgage payment at the end of the year.

3. If you have a 15 year mortgage and make bi-weekly mortgage payments you should finish paying off your mortgage in approximately 13 years and 5 months.

4. Principal payments are payments that go towards lowering your total mortgage debt or total loan balance. Interest is the cost of the money the bank has lent you for the purchase of the home.

CHAPTER 4

How Anthony and Joan paid off their mortgage in 13 years by making an additional annual payment of $3,000

"A man in debt is a man in chains."

James Lendall Basford

Anthony and Joan were both realtors and a happy couple but they could never agree on what was most important to them. Joan wanted to get a 15 year mortgage and Anthony wanted a 30 year fixed mortgage. Anthony wanted to keep the payments as low as possible because of their fluctuating income that was never a consistent amount since it was based on commissions. He said he would prefer to make additional payments every year and have a low monthly payment. Joan agreed on making additional payments but didn't want to pay the interest on the mortgage for 30 years. After considering the amount of interest they would end up paying on a 30 year mortgage, Anthony decided the 15 year mortgage was a much better option and didn't argue any more.

How it worked out

Anthony and Joan's 15 year mortgage looked like this:

They bought a home for $300,000.

They got financing in the form of a 95% mortgage: $285,000.

Which means they put a down payment of 5% which is $15,000.

Their 15 year monthly mortgage payments at a rate of 4.5% are $2,180, but they decided to make an extra payment of $3,000 every year to pay off their mortgage sooner.

Calculating your amortization schedule

Let's consider the interest being paid over the years on a 15 year mortgage since making additional annual payments can have a very positive effect when paying off debt.

We are now going to look at the amortization schedule for this loan which is basically how much of their mortgage debt was paid off each year.

With their additional annual payment of $3,000, their total mortgage debt at the end of each year is approximately:

Assuming they start making payments in April.

Year 1: $268,384

Year 2: $251,004

Year 3: $232,826

Year 4: $213,813

Year 5: $193,926

Year 6: $173,126

Year 7: $151,370

Year 8: $128,615

Year 9: $104,814

Year 10: $79,920

Year 11: $53,882

Year 12: $26,649

Year 13: $0

(Mortgage is paid off in full.)

Assuming there is no prepayment penalty for paying off the mortgage before the loan matures.

How much interest was paid when making an additional annual principal payment of $3,000?

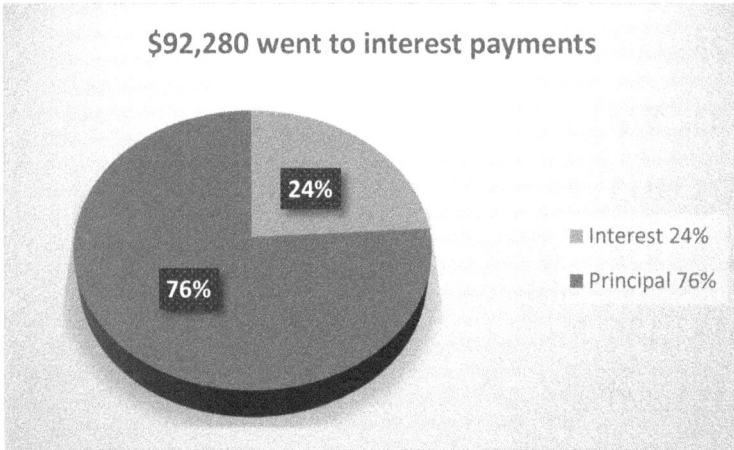

$92,280 went to interest payments

24%

76%

Interest 24%
Principal 76%

By paying off your mortgage in 13 years you would have paid $92,280 in interest. This means 24% of your payments went towards interest and 76% towards principal. If you decided not to make an additional annual payment of $3,000 towards principal you would have paid 3% more in interest payments.

On a 15 year mortgage you pay 27% in interest payments over the life of the loan.

27% - 24% = 3%

This reduction in interest payments resulted in paying off the mortgage debt in 13 years instead of 15 years.

How much did you save in interest payments if you compared this to not making any additional annual payments and if you had a 30 year mortgage instead of a 15 year mortgage?

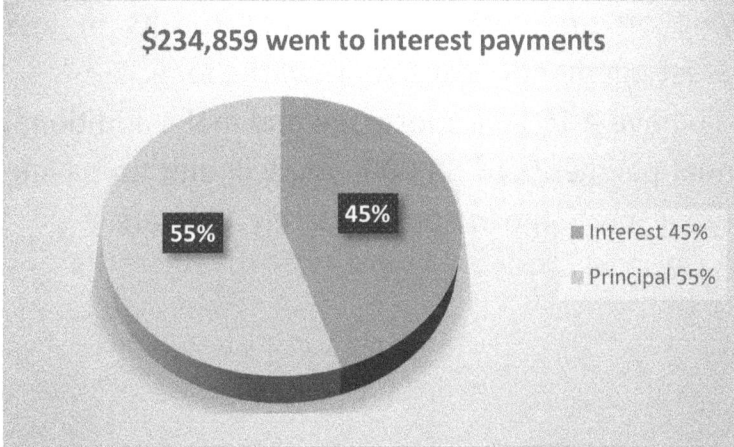

$234,859 went to interest payments

55%   45%

■ Interest 45%
■ Principal 55%

By paying off your mortgage in 30 years and made no additional payments you would have paid **$234,859 in interest which means 45% of your payments went towards interest** and 55% towards principal. Remember: Principal payments are payments that go towards lowering your total mortgage debt or total loan balance.

By making a $3,000 additional annual principal payment on a 15 year mortgage you would save 21% in interest payments over the life of the loan.

45% - 24% = 21% in savings.

KEY POINTS TO REMEMBER

1. When you make additional principal payments to pay down your debt, you will always finish paying off your mortgage sooner.
2. Paying off your mortgage sooner results in less interest payments over the life of the loan.
3. If you have a 15 year mortgage and make additional annual payments of $3,000, you will end up paying off your mortgage in approximately 13 years.

CHAPTER 5

How Vanessa and Adrian paid off their mortgage in 12 years by making an additional annual payment of $5,000

"There's nothing as short as short-term debt."

Evan Esar

Vanessa and Adrian were two big-time spenders that wanted to change their lives by eliminating their bad spending habits and buy their home. Adrian smoked two packs of cigarettes a day and Vanessa loved to eat in fancy restaurants. This had effected their health and their love life. They truly had good intentions but didn't know how to make a change. It was time to make some sacrifices. He stopped smoking and they stopped eating out in order to save enough for a down payment on a new house. Within a year they had saved enough and found a house near where they rented. Vanessa and Adrian were so proud of themselves for having committed to their goals, that they took it a step further and decided they would purchase their home with a 15 year mortgage and do what was necessary to pay it off fast. They agreed to make an additional payment of $5,000 every year. Whatever amount they were able to save passed this, they would reward themselves with a lavish night out or a small vacation depending on how much they had saved passed the $5,000.

Vanessa and Adrian cut all unnecessary spending, focused on energy savings (lower electric bill), hired an accountant to help them lowering their taxes, had a garage sale and sold all the stuff they didn't use any more (It's amazing how much you can accumulate over time). They even put all the loose change they had every day into a large water bottle that grew to about $1,500 by the end of the year. With all these savings they ended up with roughly $6,000 or more every year. Which means they passed their goal of $5,000 saved and were able to treat themselves to nice vacations and fancy restaurants with the extra cash.

How it worked out for Vanessa and Adrian

Their 15 year mortgage looked like this:

They paid $300,000 for their new home.

They financed 95% of the value of the house which was: $285,000.

They gave a down payment of 5% which is $15,000 out of pocket.

Their monthly mortgage payments with an interest rate of 4.5% rate was $2,180.

Now let's consider the interest being paid over the years on a 15 year mortgage.

With an amortization schedule calculator we are going to figure out just how much their mortgage debt went down every year. With the additional annual principal payment of $5,000, their total loan amount at the end of each year is approximately:

Assuming they start making payments in April.

Year 1: $266,384

Year 2: $246,912

Year 3: $226,546

Year 4: $205,244

Year 5: $182,964

Year 6: $159,660

Year 7: $135,286

Year 8: $109,792

Year 9: $83,126

Year 10: $55,236

Year 11: $26,064

Year 12: $0 **(Mortgage is paid off in full.)**

Assuming there is no prepayment penalty for paying off the mortgage before the loan matures.

How much interest was paid at the end of the loan?

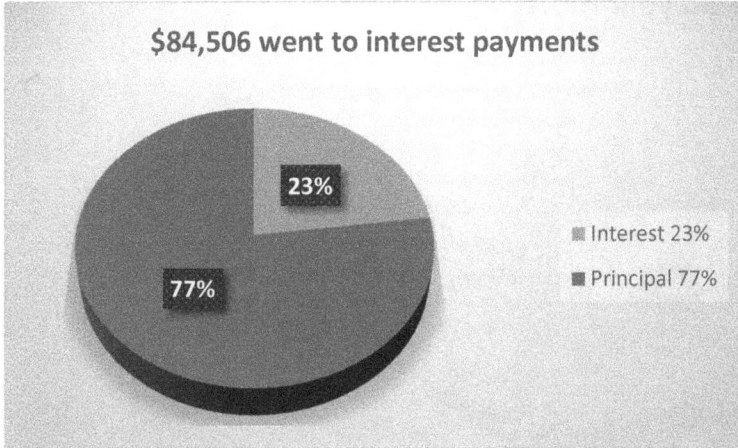

$84,506 went to interest payments

23%

77%

Interest 23%
Principal 77%

By paying off your mortgage in 12 years you would have paid $84,506 in interest which means only 23% of your payments went towards interest and 77% towards principal. You save 4% in interest payments when you make $5,000 in additional annual principal payments at the end of the life of a 15 year mortgage.

$107,442 - $84,506 = $22,936

You saved $22,936 in interest payments over the life of the loan which you can use to increase your savings, start a business, or invest in something that will benefit you in the future.

How much was saved in interest payments by not getting a 30 year mortgage?

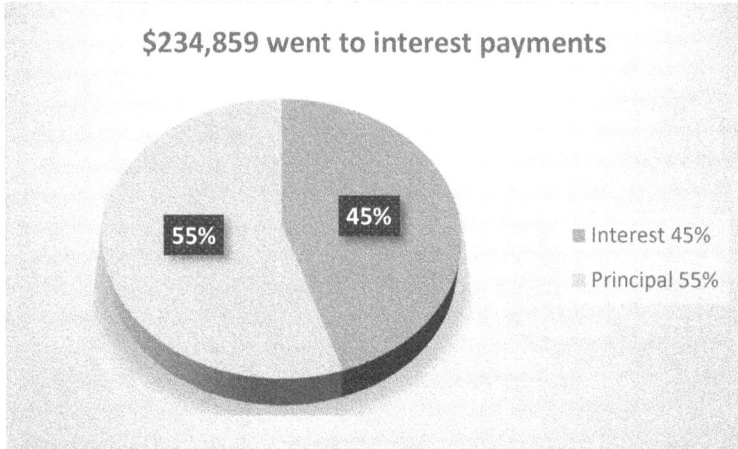

$234,859 went to interest payments

55% 45%

■ Interest 45%
▨ Principal 55%

When you get a 30 year mortgage you pay **$234,859 in interest. This equates to 45% of your payments going towards interest** and 55% going towards principal.

When you have a 15 year mortgage you end up paying $107,442 in interest payments over the life of the loan. When you have a 15 year mortgage and make $5,000 in additional annual principal payments you end up paying only $84,506 in interest payments at the end of the life of the loan.

30 year vs 15 year

$234,859 - $107,442 = **$127,417** in interest savings when you have a 15 year mortgage versus a 30 year mortgage.

What would you do with an extra $127,417?

30 year vs 15 year (with $5,000 in additional annual principal payments)

$234,859 - $84,506 = **$150,353** in interest savings when you have a 15 year mortgage and make $5,000 in additional annual principal payments versus a 30 year mortgage. This is about 22% in interest savings.

What would you do with an extra $150,353?

KEY POINTS TO REMEMBER

1. If you make additional principal payments at the end of each year of $5,000, you will finish paying off your mortgage in 12 years when you have a 15 year mortgage.
2. Making additional annual payments will not lower your mortgage payments nor your interest rate, it will only allow you to pay off the debt sooner.
3. Creating the habit of making additional payments every year is very important so that you don't skip a year here and there and end up paying off your mortgage much later.
4. Not everyone can make 15 year mortgage payments and still save enough to make additional payments at the end of the year but if you find a way to save on other things and prioritize expenses, you will find a way to make it happen.
5. Paying off your mortgage in 12 years will mean you have more years to save for retirement and more time to spend doing what you love.

CHAPTER 6

Bill's method of paying off your mortgage and all other debts in 10 years and 6 additional monthly payments

"Debt is beautiful only after it is repaid."

Russian Proverb

Bill lives down the street in a nice house. It's not a fancy house but it's very well located and has a beautiful yard to grow herbs and vegetables. Bill figured out a way to refinance his home and get out of credit card debt. He figured that if he had enough equity in his home he could eliminate his credit card payments and lower his total monthly payments. **Equity is: Appraised value – total debt after adding the credit card or personal debt to the mortgage debt and all other costs.** By refinancing his mortgage and include all personal debt (including credit cards) into the mortgage he would eliminate payments and save money. If he finished paying off his mortgage he would essentially have paid off his credit cards as well or if he sold his home at the same appraised value or higher, the credit cards would be paid off all together.

How it can work for you

Paying off your mortgage and all other debts in 10 years and 6 additional monthly payments (In this example, we are assuming Bill is refinancing to a 15 year mortgage) will require that you make additional monthly or annual principal payments by applying the credit card payment savings from having refinanced and now having only one mortgage payment.

Assuming you owe about $30,000 in credit cards and have a monthly credit card payment of $750, you can choose to include your credit card debt into your mortgage (if you have enough equity in your home). In a sense, you are consolidating debt but at a much lower interest rate (Under normal conditions.) and for a longer time frame which will mean you will finish paying off all your debts in one payment.

By using the money you are saving by not having to pay your credit cards every month you can make additional principal mortgage payments of about $750. The $750 in credit cards payments you would normally be paying every month are now used to pay down your mortgage debt which will allow you to pay off your mortgage much sooner.

Bill's step by step process

If Bill would have had a 30 year mortgage of $285,000 and refinanced to include all credit card debt totaling $30,000. After 2 years of property appreciation and a total mortgage debt of $275,593 and an appraised value of $350,000 (During a non-recession economy where the housing market is not declining.), he would have a new mortgage of approximately $306,000 assuming he refinanced the loan with a low or no closing cost loan option that many banks offer.

Originally the 30 year mortgage payment was $1,444 per month and credit card payments were $750 for a total of $2,194.

Bill's total debt payments were mortgage plus credit cards:

$1,444 + $750 = $2,194

If he refinanced to a 30 year mortgage his monthly payment would be $1,550. His would now be saving $644 every month!

$2,194 - $1,550 = $644

Wow, that's excellent but he still has to make payments for 30 years.

By refinancing to a 15 year mortgage with an interest rate of 4.5%, Bill's new mortgage payment was $2,341 which is a higher payment than the 30 year option but a smarter long term decision.

If you compare what he was paying before in mortgage credit payments ($2,194) with what he is paying now ($2,341) you would see that there is only a difference of $147 which is not a significant increase in payments but a big difference in savings over time.

By making the decision to apply the credit card payment savings back into his mortgage every month ($750) or every year ($9,000) he would pay off his mortgage in approximately 10 years and 6 additional monthly payments.

Bill knew that paying off his credit cards could take him much longer and refinancing at a reasonable interest rate would benefit him over the years. He was right. He paid off his mortgage and credit cards in 10.6 years.

Applying Bills' approach to your own situation

This is a great way to approach debt payoff since you could essentially finish paying off both your mortgage and credit cards in a few years.

Consider typical credit card rates ranging from 12-24% and your current mortgage rate of 4.5 at the time of writing this book. It's a no-brainer, you know it makes financial sense. Take the necessary steps to make it happen!

OPTION 1: PAYING OFF YOUR MORTGAGE AND CREDIT CARDS IN 15 YEARS.

This is how your 15 year refinanced mortgage would look:

Say you bought a home for $350,000 and it's now worth $382,500 after some years of appreciation have gone by.

You obtain financing in the form of an 80% loan-to-value mortgage based on the appraised value shown above for $382,500:

$382,500 x 80% = $306,000

Or

$306,000/$382,500 = 80%

The $306,000 will include all your mortgage and credit card debt as well as closing costs.

You included your credit card debt of $30,000 which means you only have mortgage debt now.

Your monthly mortgage payments with a 4.5% rate are now: $2,341

Now let's see how your debt will amortize over time when you use the credit card savings to bring down your total debt ($750 x 12 = $9,000 total which you have set aside each month in a separate bank account) to see how long it would take to pay off the mortgage loan. The approximate figures are:

Assuming you start making payments in April.

Let's look at the amortization schedule to see how the mortgage debt was paid off each year.

Year 1: $282,380

Year 2: $257,676

Year 3: $231,836

Year 4: $204,809

Year 5: $176,541

Year 6: $146,974

Year 7: $116,049

Year 8: $83,703

Year 9: $49,871

Year 10: $14,485

Year 10 (plus 6 months of payments): $0 **(Mortgage is paid off in full.)**

Assuming there is no prepayment penalty for paying off the mortgage before the loan matures.

How much interest was paid?

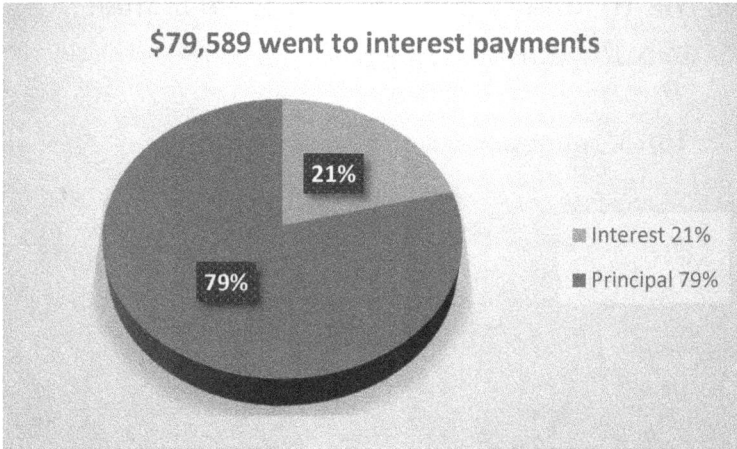

$79,589 went to interest payments

21%

79%

Interest 21%

Principal 79%

By paying off your mortgage in 10 years and 6 additional payments you would have paid only $79,589 in interest which means only 21% of your payments went towards interest and 79% towards principal.

How much did you save in interest payments if you compared this to not making any additional annual payments on a 15 year mortgage?

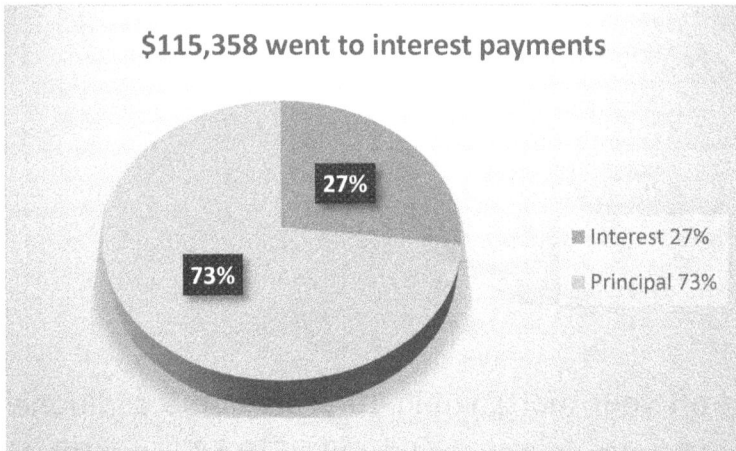

$115,358 went to interest payments

27%

73%

Interest 27%
Principal 73%

By paying off your mortgage in 15 years and made **no additional payments** you would have paid **$115,358 in interest which means 27% of your payments went towards interest** and 73% towards principal.

If you made $9,000 in additional principal payments every year you would save $35,769 or 6% in interest over the life of the loan.

OPTION 2: PAYING OFF YOU MORTGAGE AND CREDIT CARDS IN 30 YEARS.

This is how your 30 year refinanced mortgage would look:

Say you bought a home for $350,000 which is now worth $382,500.

You obtained financing in the form of 80% mortgage based on the appraised value shown above for $382,500:

$382,500 x 80% = $306,000

Or

$306,000/$382,500 = $306,000

You included your credit card debt of $30,000 which means you only have mortgage debt now.

Your monthly mortgage payments with a 4.5% rate are would be: $1,550

Now let's see how your debt will amortize over time when you use the credit card savings to bring down your total debt every year ($750 x 12 = $9,000 total which you have set aside each month in a separate bank account) to see how long it will take you to pay off your mortgage.

The approximate figures are:

Assuming you start making payments in April.

Year 1: $292,064

Year 2: $277,487

Year 3: $262,240

Year 4: $246,294

Year 5: $229,614

Year 6: $212,169

Year 7: $193,922

Year 8: $174,836

Year 9: $154,874

Year 10: $133,995

Year 11: $112,157

Year 12: $89,315

Year 13: $65,424

Year 14: $40,436

Year 15: $14,299

Year 15 (plus 9 months of payments): $0 **(Mortgage is paid off in full.)**

How much interest was paid in 30 years making $9,000 additional annual principal payments?

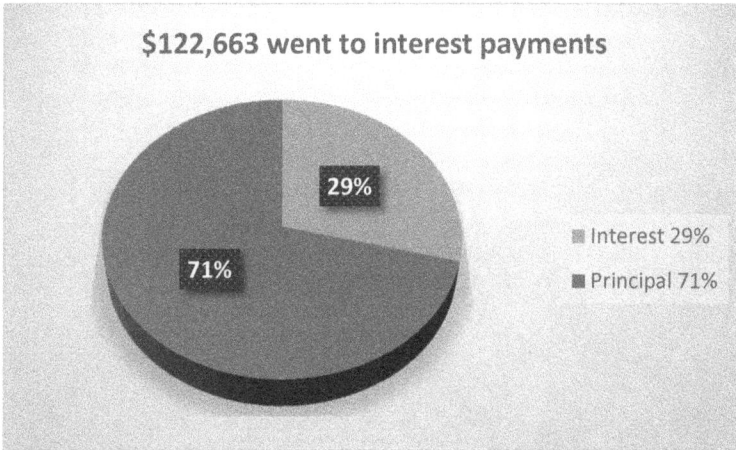

$122,663 went to interest payments

29%

71%

■ Interest 29%

■ Principal 71%

By paying off your mortgage in 15 years and 9 months you would have paid only $122,663 in interest which means only 29% of your payments went towards interest and 71% towards principal.

This greatly reduced the amount of interest you paid over time and the total time it took you to pay off your mortgage.

How much did you save in interest payments if you compared this to not making any additional annual payments towards principal on a 30 year mortgage?

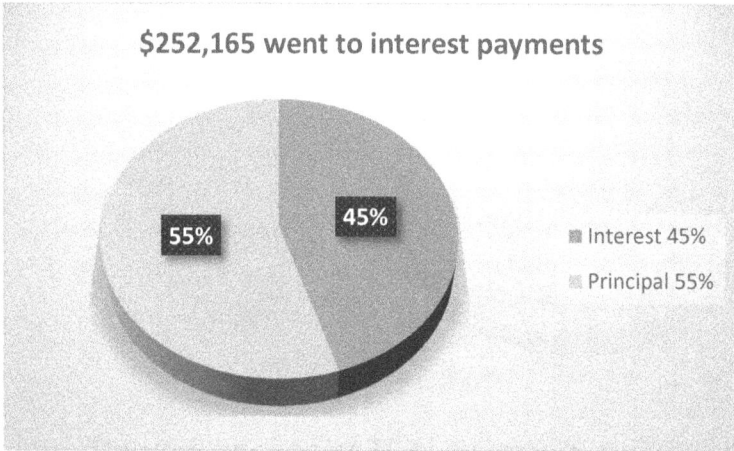

$252,165 went to interest payments

55%   45%

■ Interest 45%
■ Principal 55%

By paying off your mortgage in 30 years and made no additional payments you would have paid $252,165 in interest which means 45% of your payments went towards interest and 55% towards principal.

With this option you would have paid $129,502 in additional interest payments if you chose not to make $9,000 in annual principal payments over the life of the loan.

KEY POINTS TO REMEMBER

1. Paying off credit cards is important to your long term financial goals.

2. If you have the cash to pay off your credit cards and still have enough savings, choose to eliminate credit card debt immediately.

3. Refinancing might affect the rate you currently have but in the long term it should benefit if you are paying off both credit card and mortgage debt.

4. Having only one mortgage payment instead of having mortgage payments and credit card payments is always better.

5. Refinancing to a 15 year mortgage can make good financial sense if you can afford the payments. Normally, 15 year mortgage rates are much lower than 30 year mortgage rates which can reduce the years it takes you to pay off your mortgage but for simplicity reasons I have used a constant rate of 4.5% since rates will continue to fluctuate over time.

CHAPTER 7

Paying off your mortgage using insurance savings

"If you do not change direction, you may end up where you are heading."

Lao Tzu

If you own a house you should have insurance for your house and if you have a mortgage, the bank or lender will require that you have insurance on your house. For this reason, shopping around for rates and knowing what to ask for will make all the difference in the world. One important element of insurance payments is the deductible. Ask your bank what the maximum deductibles are and then call your insurance agent to find out what your new payments would be based on the maximum deductibles. Often you will save anywhere from $500 to $3,500 or more depending on the value of your home, which you can use to pay down your mortgage on an annual basis. Simply, put the cash you have saved into a separate interest earning savings account and at the end of the year make an extra payment towards your mortgage to bring it down and finish paying it off sooner.

Let's assume you saved $1,500 by increasing your deductibles and by shopping around for a lower payment.

Another way to lower your insurance payments is to find out if your insurance agent is using the appraised value of your home or the cost of rebuilding the property after it is destroyed to determine your payments. They should not be using the appraised value as this can often be a much higher value and will cost you a lot more to insure.

This amount can vary by large amounts so for example purposes we will use the first discount we mentioned which is having a higher deductible that can result in a significant discount in payment to determine your annual savings which in this case is $1,500.

How it can work for you

For a home worth $300,000 and current mortgage debt of $285,000 your payment would be $2,180 on a 15 year mortgage with an interest rate of 4.5%.

With an additional annual payment of $1,500 which you have saved, your mortgage debt will be eliminated in 14 years.

How great is this? You are paying off your mortgage 1 year and 1 month in advance simply because you made some calls and got a lower insurance payment and then used the savings to apply them back into your mortgage. You now have 1 year and 1 month you didn't have before to start enjoying life without mortgage payments.

Let's look at the amortization schedule to see how the mortgage debt was paid off each year.

Assuming you start making payments in April.

Year 1: $269,884

Year 2: $254,073

Year 3: $237,536

Year 4: $220,239

Year 5: $202,148

Year 6: $183,225

Year 7: $163,433

Year 8: $142,732

Year 9: $121,080

Year 10: $98,433

Year 11: $74,746

Year 12: $49,971

Year 13: $24,057

Year 14: $0 **(Mortgage is paid off in full.)**

Assuming there is no prepayment penalty for paying off the mortgage before the loan matures.

How much interest was paid?

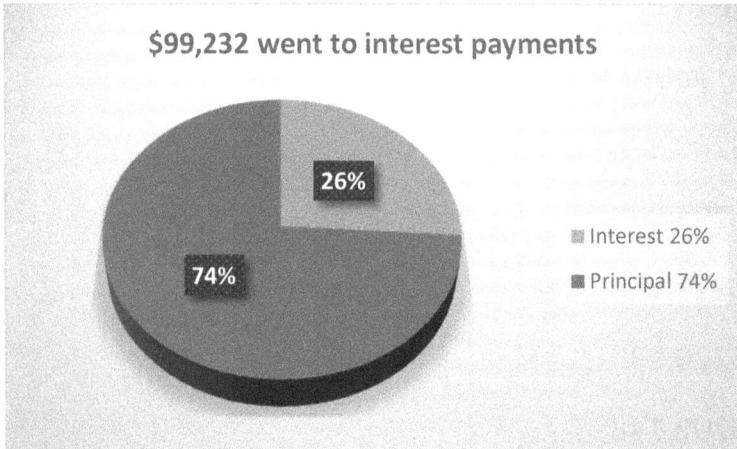

$99,232 went to interest payments

26%

74%

Interest 26%
Principal 74%

By paying off your mortgage in 14 years, you would have paid only $99,232 in interest which means only 26% of your payments went towards interest and 74% towards principal.

You saved yourself a year of interest payments by simply making some calls and finding out what will benefit you the most. It's worth it. Get on the phone or go see your insurance agent. Their might be even more discounts you qualify for.

How much did you save in interest payments when comparing a 30 year mortgage with a 15 year mortgage where you made additional annual principal payments?

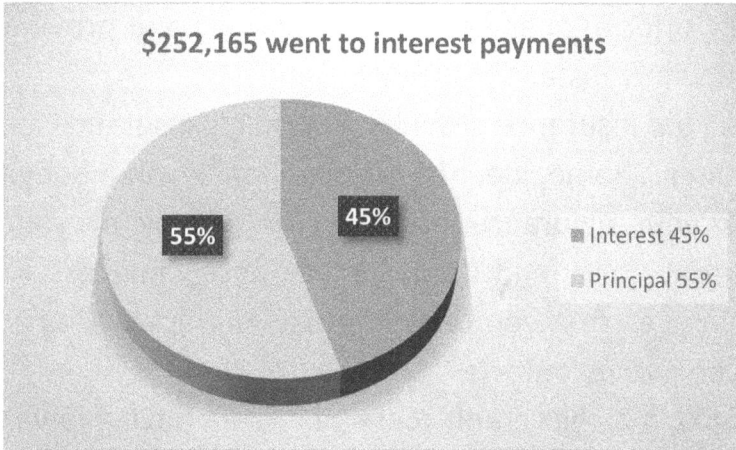

$252,165 went to interest payments

55%   45%

■ Interest 45%
■ Principal 55%

If you had a 30 year mortgage and paid it off at the end of the 30 years and made no additional principal payments you would have paid **$252,165 in interest over the life of the loan. This means 45% of your payments went towards interest** and 55% towards principal.

Let's compare this to a 15 year mortgage with $1,500 in additional annual principal payments

$252,165 - $99,232 = $152,933 is what you saved in interest payments by having a 15 year mortgage and by making $1,500 in additional annual principal payments.

KEY POINTS TO REMEMBER

1. Shopping around for the lowest insurance payments is very important. Make sure to ask what discounts they offer as these can add up quickly and provide you with substantial savings.

2. Ask your insurance provider if bundling insurance for your car, home, life, and other will save you money.

3. Ask your insurance provider for a copy of your current policy and decide if you have unnecessary coverages that you can eliminate and actually save some money on.

4. Having a higher credit score can mean having lower insurance payments so make sure you work on improving your credit by paying off debt and paying on time.

5. Sometimes, insurance companies offer discounts when you pay your bill in full instead of making monthly payments. This is an easy way to lower your payments.

CHAPTER 8

Paying off your mortgage using property tax savings

"What can be added to the happiness of a man who is in health, out of debt, and has a clear conscience?"

Adam Smith

Property taxes are determined by your local tax jurisdiction. It often grants tax exemptions that you may qualify for under certain circumstances, such as: homestead exemption, elderly exemption, veteran's exemption, etc. When you pay in advance (in some tax jurisdictions) you can also get additional savings. These savings can vary depending on the value of your home and the type of exemption you get. This is one way to lower your property taxes.

Another way to lower you property taxes is to dispute the tax assessed value through an appeal process specific to your area (if you feel the tax assessed value is wrong). It is always better to consult with a real estate attorney who specializes in this process as they can save you a considerable amount in taxes and often charge a percentage of what they save you.

A third way to lower your property taxes is to challenge property taxes if your tax jurisdiction has incorrect information regarding your home such as: square footage, acreage, property features, etc.

For example, let's assume you saved $2,000 by disputing the tax assessed value of your home and applied a specific exemption as well, particular to your situation. This amount can be higher or lower depending on the value of your home but we will use $2,000 for example purposes.

How these savings can work for you

For a home appraised at $300,000 and a mortgage of $285,000 your monthly payment would be $2,180 on a 15 year mortgage with an interest rate of 4.5%.

If you applied the $2,000 you saved in property taxes towards your mortgage as an additional annual principal payment, your mortgage debt will be eliminated in 13 years and 7 months.

Now let's consider how this will benefit you. You are paying off your mortgage 1 year and 5 months early simply because you researched and made some calls and then applied the savings to the mortgage.

Using an amortization schedule calculator we can figure out how much of your mortgage was paid off each year.

Assuming you start making payments in April.

Year 1: $269,384

Year 2: $253,050

Year 3: $235,966

Year 4: $218,097

Year 5: $199,407

Year 6: $179,859

Year 7: $159,412

Year 8: $138,026

Year 9: $115,658

Year 10: $92,262

Year 11: $67,791

Year 12: $42,197

Year 13: $15,426

Year 13 (plus 7 months of payments): $0

(Mortgage is paid off in full.)

Assuming there is no prepayment penalty for paying off the mortgage before the loan matures.

How much interest was paid?

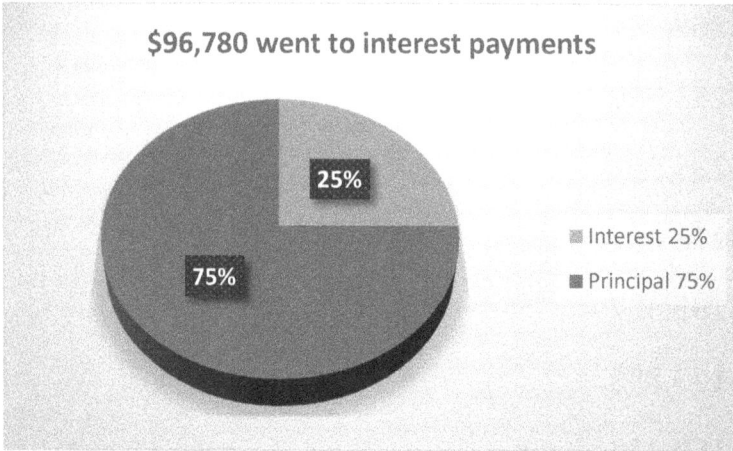

$96,780 went to interest payments

25%

75%

Interest 25%

Principal 75%

By making an additional annual principal payment of $2,000 on a 15 year mortgage you would be able to pay off your mortgage in 13 years and 7 months. This means you would have only paid $96,780 in interest over the life of the loan. Only 25% of your payments went towards interest.

How much did you save in interest by making $2,000 in additional annual principal payments on a 15 year mortgage versus having a 30 year mortgage?

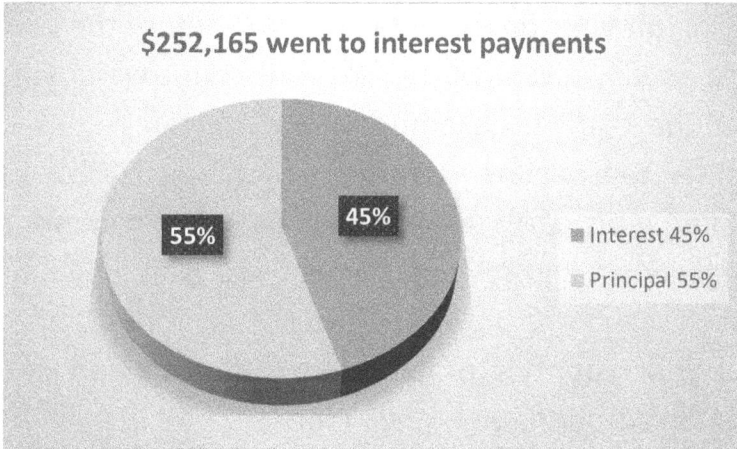

$252,165 went to interest payments

55% | 45%

Interest 45%
Principal 55%

By paying off your mortgage in 30 years you would have paid **$252,165 in interest. Since you only paid $96,780 on your 15 year mortgage, you saved $155,385.**

On a 30 year mortgage, 45% of your payments are going towards interest and on a 15 year mortgage only 25% went to interest which saved you 20% over the life of the loan. Great job!

There are so many things you could do with the $155,385 you saved in interest.

Call a real estate attorney and see just how much you could save on property taxes.

KEY POINTS TO REMEMBER

1. Always check your county or tax jurisdiction website to see what exemptions they offer.
2. Paying off your property taxes in full before the due date usually gives you the most discount when you don't have any tax exemptions.
3. Call a real estate attorney who specializes in disputing property taxes as they can offer you more suggestions, and save you time if you plan on doing this.
4. Call your county's property tax office to find out what exemptions you qualify for.

CHAPTER 9

Paying off your mortgage in 9 years and 9 additional monthly payments using the combined savings method

"Debt is your friend in times of abundance, and your enemy in times of scarcity."

Unknown

After reading the previous chapters you now know there are great options available to you when creating a mortgage savings plan. These options will allow you to pay off your mortgage sooner than what most banks propose. Paying a mortgage for 30 years should be the last thing you do if you have other alternatives. Plan to pay less in debts and save more for the future. Your largest debt is your mortgage. Having a 15 year mortgage instead of a 30 year mortgage allows you to pay off debt much sooner.

Let's go over all the areas in your finances that you could be benefiting from and prepare a possible scenario of what you could be doing:

Combined savings methods

Assuming your new mortgage loan amount after refinancing and including all credit card debt is $306,000 and you have a 15 year mortgage with an interest rate of 4.5%.

Your bi-weekly mortgage payments would be $1,170.

Tax savings: $2,000

Insurance savings: $1,500

Additional annual payments from simply cost-cutting and saving: $5,000

Credit card savings: $750

Bi-weekly payment savings resulting in additional annual payments of: $2,341 (rounded up)

Total savings that will be added in the form of an annual payment: $9,250

Including the bi-weekly payment annual savings of $2,341 the total additional annual principal payments you would be: $11,591

How this method can work for you

With an additional principal payment of $11,591 (including total savings and bi-weekly payment annual result) which you have saved, your mortgage debt would be eliminated in 9 years and 9 months.

This is a big deal. You will be very proud of yourself for being in the top percent of homeowners who finish paying off their mortgage sooner than the rest. You are paying off your mortgage 20 years and 3 months earlier simply because you found a way to save and reduced expenses and then applied those savings to your mortgage.

Let's look at the amortization schedule to see how the mortgage debt was paid off each year.

Assuming you start making payments in April.

Year 1: $279,789

Year 2: $252,375

Year 3: $223,700

Year 4: $193,709

Year 5: $162,340

Year 6: $129,529

Year 7: $95,212

Year 8: $59,317

Year 9: $21,774

Year 9 (plus 9 months of payments): $0 **(Mortgage is paid off in full.)**

Assuming there is no prepayment penalty for paying off the mortgage before the loan matures.

How much interest was paid using combined savings methods?

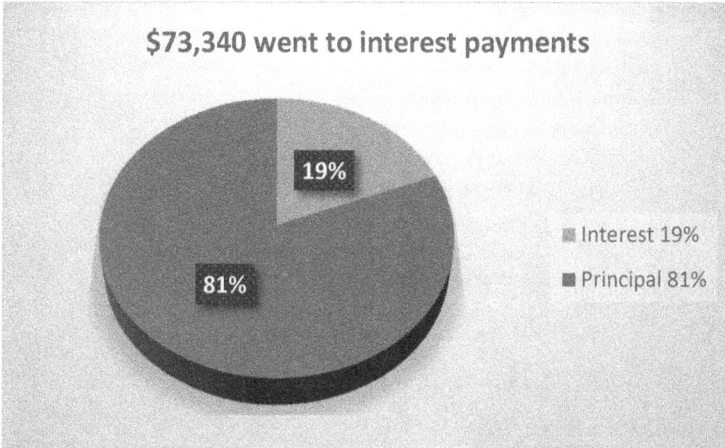

$73,340 went to interest payments

19%

81%

Interest 19%
Principal 81%

You would have paid only $73,340 in interest when paying off your mortgage in 9 years and 9 additional monthly payments which means only 19% of your payments went towards interest and 81% towards principal. These are substantial savings when comparing this option to simply paying it off in 30 years or even 15 years with no additional principal payments.

How much money did you save in interest payments if you compared the combined savings method on a 15 year mortgage to a 30 year mortgage?

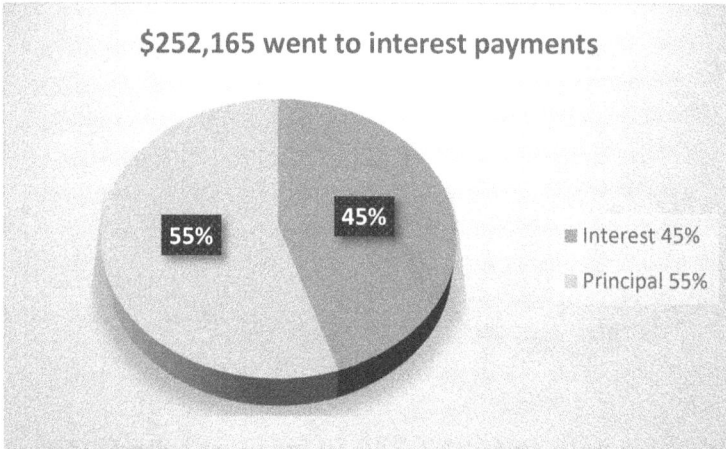

$252,165 went to interest payments

55%

45%

■ Interest 45%

■ Principal 55%

By paying off your mortgage in 30 years and making no additional payments you would pay $252,165 in interest compared to $73,340 when using the combined savings method. This would mean you would be saving $178,825 in interest payments over the life of the loan. This would be a major difference when paying off your mortgage. On a 30 year mortgage, 45% of your payments would go towards interest, but in the combined savings method you would only make 19% of your payments towards interest. That's 26% in savings.

$252,165 - $73,340 = $178,825 in interest savings

KEY POINTS TO REMEMBER

1. To get the maximum interest savings possible, you will need to combine all savings methods.
2. Saving and prioritizing your expenses will result in having a sound financial future.
3. Don't worry if you can't apply all the savings mentioned. Simply, do your best to save as much as possible and apply those savings to your mortgage.

CHAPTER 10

Paying off your mortgage in just over 8 years using the combined savings method and rental income of $500 per month

"Be assured that it gives much more pain to the mind to be in debt, than to do without any article whatever which we may seem to want."

Thomas Jefferson

A great alternative to increasing the amount of money you can apply towards your mortgage payments is renting space in your house. If you have a guest house, an extra room, an efficiency, or any other legitimate living space in your home, you can rent that space to bring in extra cash.

Depending on the area where you may live and what rent is going for, you could be bringing in a decent amount of money which will greatly reduce your mortgage debt if applied towards paying down your mortgage. You can apply the income you receive from rent to your mortgage on a monthly or annual basis. Over the years you will start to see the positive effects this can have on bringing down what you owe the bank. Once you finish paying off your mortgage, you can either stop renting out space in your home or continue to receive these extra payments. College students are a great option as renters since they often have to spend most of their day in school and then need to study the remainder of the time. Just make sure you limit who they bring to your home as they might be responsible but their friends might not.

With new websites and mobile apps that have come out these last few years, finding short-term and long-term renters has never been easier. Some examples of these websites are: Airbnb, tripping.com, flipkey, homeaway, vrbo, housetrip, etc. These are not the only online sources for finding renters and are only examples of where you can offer space for rent quickly and affordably.

How it can work for you

By using the savings from the last chapter and adding rental income we have this mortgage payment scenario:

Monthly Rental income: $500

Tax savings: $2,000

Insurance savings: $1,500

Additional annual payments from cost cutting and saving: $5,000

Credit card savings: $750

Bi-weekly payment savings resulting in additional annual payments of: $2,341 (rounded up)

Total savings that will be added in the form of an annual payment: $9,250

Including the bi-weekly payment annual savings of $2,341 the total additional annual principal payments would be: $11,591 plus $6,000 gives us a total of $17,591 (Remember, you have $500 per month from rental income which can be applied on a monthly or annual basis. Monthly would be better so that you resist the urge to spend that money on something else.).

This might sound like a large amount but when you break this down monthly it would only be $1,466 that you would be applying towards your mortgage, which is mostly from cost-cutting and rental income.

Your mortgage would basically look like this:

You would have bi-weekly payments of $1,171 on a 15 year mortgage with an interest rate of 4.5%.

Your new mortgage loan amount when refinancing and including all credit card debt would be: $306,000

Let's look at the amortization schedule to see how the mortgage debt was paid off each year.

Assuming you start making payments in April.

Year 1: $273,664

Year 2: $239,843

Year 3: $204,467

Year 4: $167,467

Year 5: $128,767

Year 6: $88,289

Year 7: $45,951

Year 8: $1,669 (1 payment of $1,669)

Year 8: $0

(Mortgage is paid off in full.)

Assuming there is no prepayment penalty for paying off the mortgage before the loan matures.

How much interest was paid using the combined savings method and $500 in additional rental income?

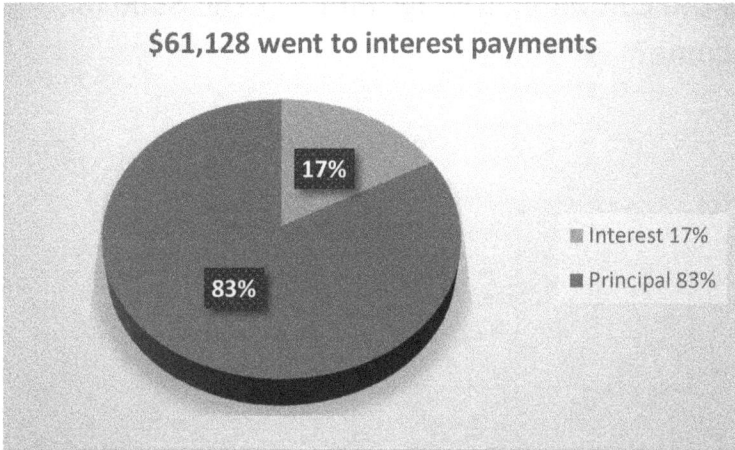

$61,128 went to interest payments

17%

83%

Interest 17%
Principal 83%

By using the combined savings method and including an additional rental income of $500 per month you would finish paying off your mortgage in 8 years plus an additional payment of $1,669.

In total, you would have paid $61,128 in interest which means only 17% of your payments went towards interest and 83% towards principal.

How much money did you save in interest payments if you compared a 30 year mortgage to a 15 year mortgage that uses the combined savings method and $500 in rental income?

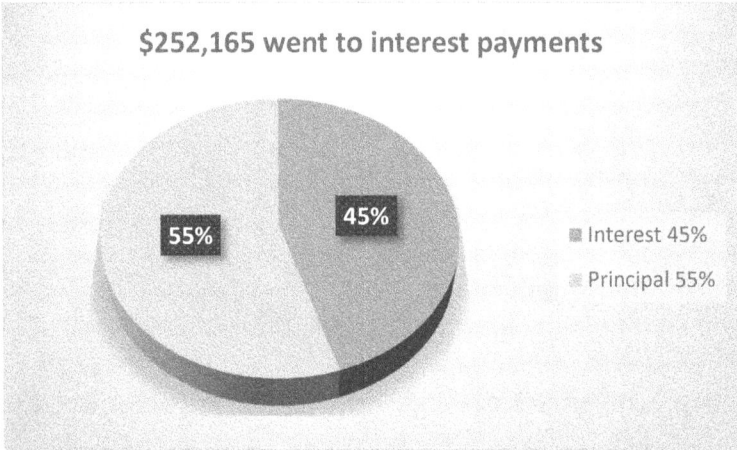

$252,165 went to interest payments

55% 45%

■ Interest 45%
■ Principal 55%

If you finish paying off your mortgage in 30 years you would pay **$252,165 in interest. On a 15 year mortgage, using the combined savings method and a rental income of $500, you would pay $61,128. You would save $191,037 in interest payments!**

$252,165 - $61,128 = $191,037

KEY POINTS TO REMEMBER

1. Sometimes a small amount of rental income can have a significant result on how fast you can pay off your mortgage.
2. $500 of rental income results in $6,000 of additional mortgage pay off funds on an annual basis.
3. Paying off your mortgage sooner will always result in saving enormous amounts of interest payments over the years.
4. Make sure to apply the rental income you receive towards your mortgage, as you might be tempted to spend it on something else.

CHAPTER 11

Paying off your mortgage in 7 years and 7 months using the combined savings method and a rental income of $750 per month

"Let every man, every corporation, and especially let every village, town, and city, every county and state, get out of debt and keep out of debt. It is the debtor that is ruined by hard times."

Rutherford B. Hayes

Who knew you could bring down so much debt in such short time. Well now you have the knowledge to do so but only if you take the necessary steps to make it happen. Collecting rent for a room or space in your home is a great way to bring extra income that you can use to pay down your mortgage with.

Let's take it a step further

If you increase your rental income to $750 you will see even greater benefits over the long haul. When renting a room or space in your home always remember to go over some basic formalities that should not be overlooked. When renting space in your home remember to:

- Always use a lease agreement.
- Ask for 1 months deposit in case of any unforeseen circumstances.
- Never forget to do a background check on all renters.
- Provide a clean and safe living environment.
- Cash the check before allowing the renter to move in to your home.
- Establish rules of conduct and anything else you think is important before they move in.

These are just a few things that can be very useful to remember and can save you a lot of trouble down the road. Most renters are great but it's always better to go through the formalities mentioned above just in case you get a renter who doesn't keep their end of the deal. For specific advice and when completing a lease agreement contact a real estate attorney as they will give you the information you need to do things right and prevent any problems in the future.

How it can work for you

Using the numbers from the last chapter but now adding $750 in rental income we have:

Rental income: $750

Tax savings: $2,000

Insurance savings: $1,500

Additional annual principal payments from cost cutting and saving: $5,000

Credit card savings: $750

Bi-weekly payment savings resulting in additional annual payments of: $2,341 (rounded up)

Total savings that will be added in the form of an annual payment: $9,250

Including the bi-weekly payment annual savings of $2,341 the total additional annual principal payments would be: $11,591 plus $9,000 gives us a total of $20,591 (Remember, you have $750 per month from rental income which can be applied on a monthly or annual basis. Monthly payments are better to prevent yourself from spending the money on something else.).

The total would be $20,591. This might sound like a large amount but when you break this down monthly it would only be $1,716 which is mostly from cost-cutting and rental income.

Your mortgage would basically look like this:

You would have bi-weekly payments of $1,171 on a 15 year mortgage with an interest rate of 4.5%.

Your new mortgage loan amount when refinancing and including all credit card debt would be $306,000.

Let's look at the amortization schedule to see how the mortgage debt was paid off each year.

Assuming you start making payments in April.

Year 1: $270,601

Year 2: $233,577

Year 3: $194,851

Year 4: $154,346

Year 5: $111,981

Year 6: $67,669

Year 7: $21,321

Year 7 (plus 7 additional payments and $6.14): $0

(Mortgage is paid off in full.)

Assuming there is no prepayment penalty for paying off the mortgage before the loan matures.

How much interest was paid?

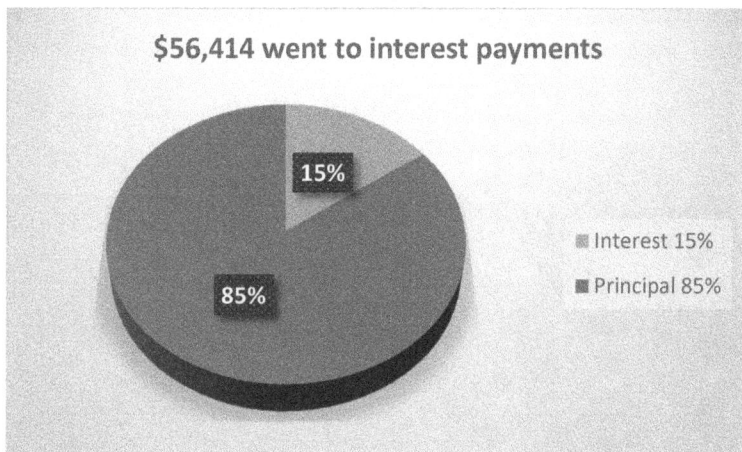

$56,414 went to interest payments

15%

85%

Interest 15%
Principal 85%

By paying off your mortgage in 7 years and 7 more payments you would have paid only $56,414 in interest.

This means only 15% of your payments went towards interest and 85% towards principal. This is big difference when comparing this to a 30 year mortgage.

How much money was saved in interest payments when comparing this with only $500 in rental income?

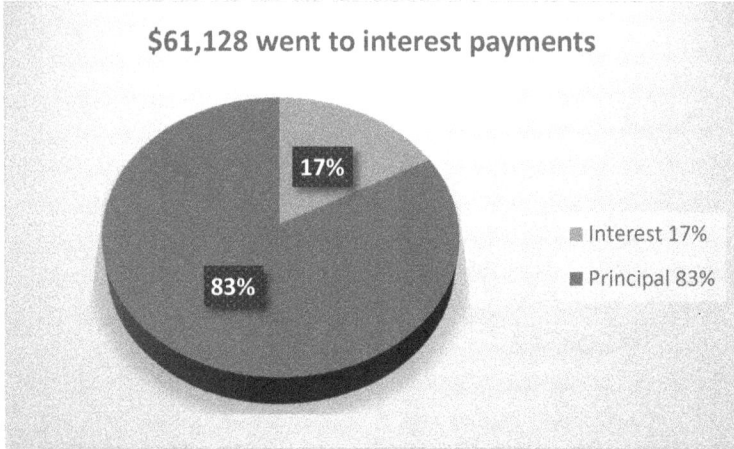

$61,128 went to interest payments

17%

83%

Interest 17%

Principal 83%

Having $750 instead of $500 in rental income comes down to saving $4,237 in interest payments.

$61,128 - $56,414 = $4,714

Even though this is only a 2% difference in savings you still reduced the amount of time it took you to pay off your mortgage.

How much money did you save in interest payments if you compared this to not making any additional annual payments and if you had a 30 year mortgage instead of a 15 year mortgage?

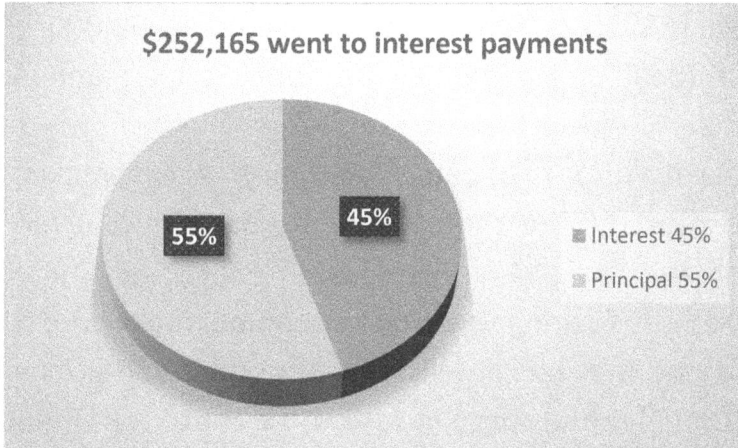

$252,165 went to interest payments

Interest 45%
Principal 55%

You total interest payments over the life of the loan on a 30 year mortgage is $252,165. If you only paid $56,414 in interest payments on a 15 year mortgage using the combined savings method and a rental income of $750, you would have saved $195,751.

KEY POINTS TO REMEMBER

1. You don't have to rent space in your house if you don't feel comfortable doing this or if you prefer to have more privacy.

2. Having $750 of rental income results in $9,000 of additional mortgage pay off funds on an annual basis.

3. Make it a priority to pay off your mortgage by making the most of the rental income you receive every month.

4. When considering to purchase a home, make sure to find one that has at least 2 bedrooms or additional potential rental space in case you want to rent it out in the future.

5. If you lose your job or start having financial problems, it's always good to have more rooms or space to rent out.

CHAPTER 12

Paying off your mortgage in 6 years and 8 months using the combined savings method and a rental income of $1,200 per month

"Only spend after you have saved."

Unknown

The benefits of being able to rent space in your home are many, but the main benefit is the ability to make additional payments to your mortgage. This allows you to pay off your debt much sooner and save substantially in interest payments. When you increase your additional principal payments by $1,200 or more per month you will see results happen very faster. By applying the combined savings method and a rental income of $1,200 you will pay down your mortgage at an accelerated rate. This will create a snowball effect that will build up over time. The key is to find good renters that can afford to make these payments.

When searching for renters you can use a number of methods that will help you find good renters in very little time.

Some ways of finding good and high paying renters are:

- Yard signs. This is my favorite for people who are interested in renting and are in the area already.
- Zillow.com is a great place to find good quality renters.
- Craigslist.com is another place to get a high volume of renters but not always will they be high quality.
- Trulia.com and rent.com are also great online options.
- Newspaper ads. This is the old fashioned way to advertise and is not used as commonly as before but it's still an option.

For short term and long term rentals you can also use:

- Airbnb.com has become very popular and is easy to use.
- Vrbo.com is also another online source for finding renters.

If you want to use social media to find renters you can always place your ad or simply let others know you are looking for:

- Facebook.com
- Twitter.com
- Instagram.com
- Youtube.com

How it can work for you

Using the numbers from the previous chapter but now adding a new rental income amount of $1,200 we have:

Rental income: $1,200

Tax savings: $2,000

Insurance savings: $1,500

Additional annual payments from cost cutting and saving: $5,000

Credit card savings: $750

Bi-weekly payment savings resulting in additional annual payments of: $2,341 (rounded up)

Total savings that will be added in the form of an annual payment: $9,250

Including the bi-weekly payment annual savings of $2,341 the total additional annual principal payments would be: $11,591 plus $14,400 ($1,200 per month from rental income which can be applied on a monthly basis or annually. Monthly payments are always better in order to prevent spending the rental income on something else.). The total would be $11,591 + 14,400 = $25,991.

When you break this amount down into monthly payments it would only be $2,166 which is mostly from cost-cutting and rental income.

Your mortgage would basically look like this:

You would have bi-weekly payments of $1,171 on a 15 year mortgage with an interest rate of 4.5%.

Your new mortgage loan amount when refinancing and including all credit card debt would be $306,000.

Let's look at the amortization schedule to see how the mortgage debt was paid off each year.

Assuming you start your payments in April.

Year 1: $265,089

Year 2: $222,298

Year 3: $177,541

Year 4: $130,728

Year 5: $81,765

Year 6: $30,552

Year 6 (plus 8 additional payments): $0

(Mortgage is paid off in full.)

Assuming there is no prepayment penalty for paying off the mortgage before the loan matures.

How much interest was paid?

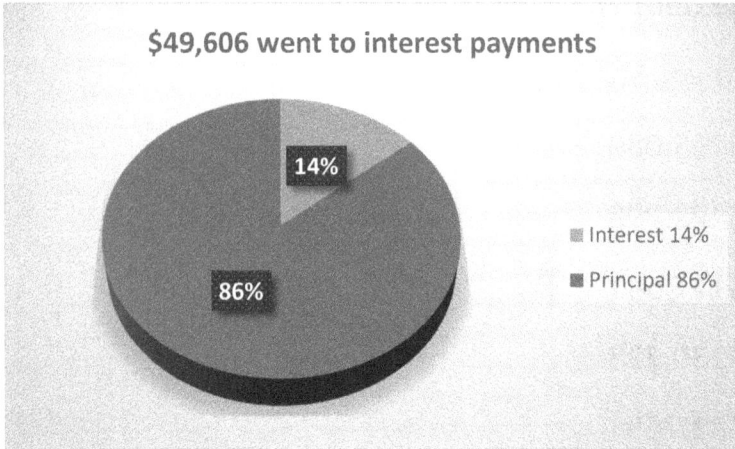

$49,606 went to interest payments

14%

86%

Interest 14%

Principal 86%

By paying off your mortgage in 6 years and 8 more payments you would have paid only $49,606 in interest which means only 14% of your payments went towards interest and 86% towards principal.

How much money was saved in interest payments when comparing with only $750 in rental income?

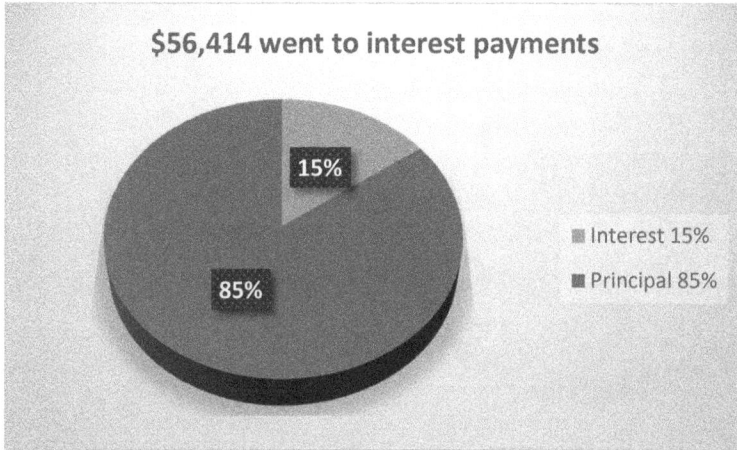

$56,414 went to interest payments

15%

85%

■ Interest 15%
■ Principal 85%

If you have a rental income of $750 you would be paying $56,414 in interest versus having $1,200 in rental income and only paying $49,606 in interest payments. This is a difference of $6,808 over the life of the loan. You would save **$6,808** by having a rental income of $1,200 instead of $750.

How much money was saved in interest payments when comparing with only $500 in rental income?

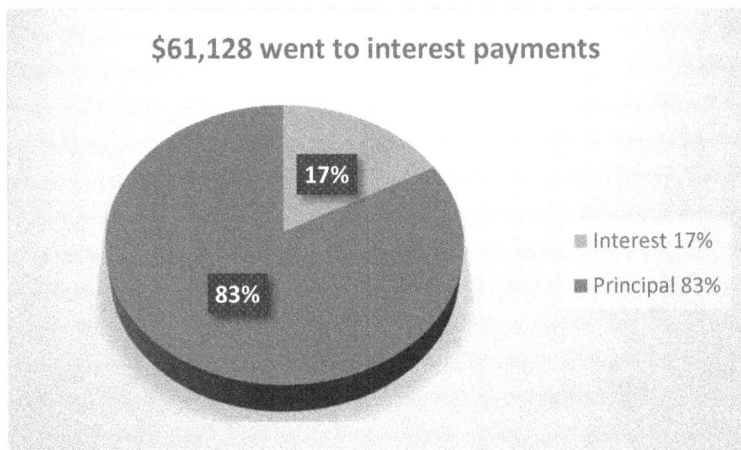

$61,128 went to interest payments

17%

83%

Interest 17%

Principal 83%

If you have a rental income of $500 you would be paying $61,128 in interest versus having $1,200 in rental income and only paying $49,606 in interest payments. This is a difference of $11,522 over the life of the loan. You would save **$11,522** by having a rental income of $1,200 instead of $500.

How much money is saved in interest payments if you have a 15 year mortgage using the combined savings method and a rental income of $1,200 instead of having a 30 year mortgage?

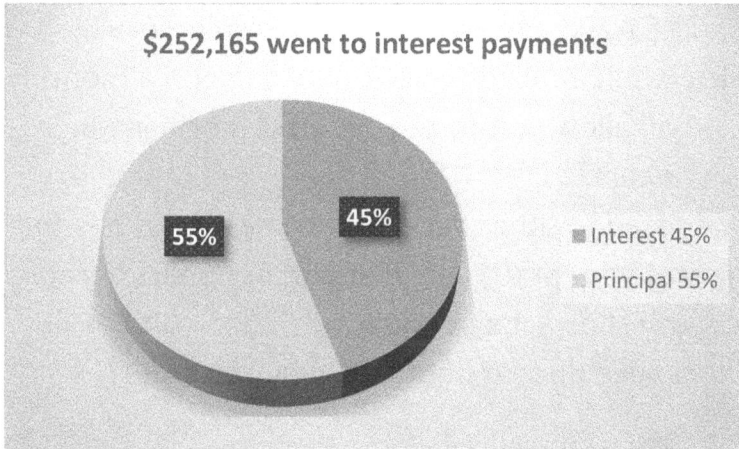

$252,165 went to interest payments

55% 45%

Interest 45%
Principal 55%

On a 30 year mortgage you would have paid $252,165 in interest over the life of the loan. On a 15 year mortgage using the combined savings method and having a rental income of $1,200, you would pay $49,606. **You would save $202,559 in interest payments over the life of the loan.**

$252,165 – 49,606 = $202,559

KEY POINTS TO REMEMBER

1. You can pay off your mortgage in 6 years and 8 months using the numbers and methods shown in this example.
2. Having $1,200 of rental income results in $14,400 which when applied to your mortgage on a monthly basis will allow you to pay off your mortgage in less than 7 years.
3. Don't listen to other people who say it's not possible to pay of your mortgage in less than 7 years because the math shows it's possible.
4. Others have done it before so why can't you?

CHAPTER 13

Putting the Plan Together

"If you want to find prosperity, run in the opposite direction of debt."

Unknown

In order to pay off your mortgage in 6-8 years we are going to put together a specific plan that needs to be executed as close as possible to make it reality. If you skip a step you can't expect to have the same results as what is being shown here. Now, let's make some magic happen.

Step 1:

Contact a bank or lender that offers a low closing cost mortgage. Make sure the rate is also reasonable so that your payments stay low. Tell them you are looking for a 15 year mortgage and want to know what they can offer based on your down payment or equity (if refinancing) and your credit score.

Step 2:

Ask the bank if they offer a bi-weekly loan program and tell them that's what you want. Most of the time banks have this option which will help make this plan possible.

Step 3:

If refinancing, tell them you want to pay off all your credit cards (maybe even include your car if you feel the payments are high or simply want one less payment a month). That way the bank can verify your credit report to calculate how much you owe and then figure out if you have enough equity to pay off all the debts you want paid off.

Step 4:

If purchasing a home, contact several insurance companies over the phone so that they can give you details of what they can offer. Once you have all their quotes, call them back and ask them if they can do better (hopefully from a trusted insurance company). If refinancing your home, do the same but call your current insurance company and ask them if they can do better than "XYZ" company. Most of the time you will save a lot of money by doing this and then do this every year since insurance payments are based on many different factors including age, credit, location based criteria (not having a hurricane or tornado in the last "x" passed years for example.). You will apply the savings in insurance payments towards your principal in the form of a principal payment every year.

Step 5:

When your next property tax payment is due you need to contact your tax jurisdiction to find out what exemptions you may qualify for and then apply the savings back into your mortgage in the form of principal payments to pay down your debt. Also, if you feel the tax assessed value that has been given to your home is wrong, contest this amount by hiring an attorney who specializes in this matter. Usually, real estate attorneys are your best option. Often times, they will charge you based on a percentage of what they save you. Attorney fees change depending on the area where you live and other factors. Make sure you call more than one attorney so that you can get the best deal..

Step 6:

Decide if you want or can rent space in your home such as an extra room, an efficiency, the guest house, etc. Collect this monthly rental income that you will then use to make additional principal payments. You really only have to do this until you finish paying off your mortgage which should be soon if you do things right. There are many companies and websites that allow you to offer your room or space for rent and you decide the terms at which its rented. Some of these companies are: Airbnb, tripping.com, flipkey, homeaway, vrbo, housetrip, etc. These are just examples so make sure to research which one is best for you. I have even seen people convert their basements or garages into rooms and made it very comfortable for tenants, just make sure you provide a safe living area.

Step 7:

If this isn't enough, get a second job or a part-time job to increase your income doing different things like: tutoring, translations, coaching a sport, baby sitting, proofreading books, raking leaves, mowing the lawn, etc. This is just an additional option to bring in income but not necessary if you see that everything else is providing sufficient savings. Over time, you will see significant changes in your finances. Once you start, you will see that it's definitely possible to pay off your mortgage much sooner than the bank proposed 30 year mortgage payment structure.

Step 8:

Celebrate once you have paid off your mortgage! Go on vacation or throw a party with friends and loved ones.

Step 9:

Help others to get out of debt by showing them how to do the same as you are doing or have done. If it's too much information, share this book with them so they can take it home and review everything at their own pace. Share the information you have learned with other people you think will benefit from it and if someone is not convinced it's possible, simply share the book and let them come around.

If more people in the world are out of debt, many positive things will happen:

- Families won't have to work as hard and will have more time to be together.
- When parents are able to spend more time with their kids they can strengthen core beliefs and develop important qualities that will benefit our society and will make happier homes.
- People will be less stressed out and will lead happier lives.
- More people will be able to go on vacations and start new ventures that will help the economy and their own lives.
- Most people will be able to save more for retirement which will mean more people can retire sooner.
- By having less payments to make, most people will have more free time and that will mean more freedom to do what you love doing.

CHAPTER 14

Never do this when getting a mortgage

"Those who are in debt learn the lesson."

Unknown

There are things you need to remember to never do when getting a mortgage from a bank or lender. If you already have any of these or are in any of these situations, there are always ways of getting out but you need to consult with your mortgage professional to find out. Most people learn the hard way which is through trial and error but if you follow these "Never-do Rules" you will save yourself time and a lot of headaches.

Never get a loan with a prepayment penalty

Prepayment penalties are fees in the form of money you will have to pay if you pay off you mortgage before a specific time period. Some banks will impose a 2-5 year prepayment period. If the loan has this penalty, the fee is usually about 3% of the loan amount which is a large amount when you're trying to pay off your loan. Make sure to ask you mortgage professional or bank representative if the loan has a prepayment penalty and if they offer mortgages that don't have penalties for paying off your mortgage sooner. Don't get a mortgage with a prepayment penalty.

Never get an interest only mortgage loan

This is only for investors or financial savvy people If you are neither of these, you will never finish paying off the loan and will have to refinance or sell your house. You don't want to make payments forever and find out you still owe the same amount you originally started with.

Never let the bank choose what day you make your mortgage payments

You should always let the bank know what day or days you want to make your mortgage payments so that they conveniently coincide with the dates when you are paid and the money is available to use for making payments. When you make bi-weekly payments you need to establish the date for both days in the month. This will help you become organized and will prevent you from making late payments.

Never get an automatic payment option

Never choose an automatic payment option, since you need to make it a habit of supervising what you are paying each month so that you can keep adding payments to the principal balance and finish paying off the mortgage. By having automatic payments withdrawn from your bank account you will:

1) Not pay as much attention to how much is going towards paying off the mortgage.

2) Forget to plan for additional mortgage principal payments.

3) Not make it a habit of searching for newer and better ways to save in other areas in order to apply more mortgage payments and pay off the loan sooner.

There is an exception to this point which is that you can have automatic payments withdrawn from your bank account when you are the type of person that will forget to make payments if it is not automatically withdrawn and in this case, you need to make sure you make the additional principal payments in an organized manner. Some people have a lot of things on their mind and might forget to make payments. Automatic payments can be an option but always prefer to make your payments without an automatic option so that you can be on top of how much goes towards paying down your mortgage every time.

Never get a co-signer or become a cosigner

Never get a co-signer or become a co-signer when getting a mortgage unless they agree to help to make the mortgage payments and understand the responsibility they are undertaking. Co-signers usually end up being family members which means that if for any reason you make late payments or end up defaulting on the loan they will also be negatively affected. If you want to maintain a good relationship with family members, don't ask them to be a co-signer on the loan.

There is an exception to this point which is that you consider the co-signer for the purchase as an investor and you are partners in the deal where both of you invest money and will have a prearranged profit percentage. This will prevent future problems. Always have this in writing.

Never refinance if the costs of refinancing will be too high

Increasing debt is not the ultimate goal and having worked hard to pay down the mortgage only to bring the loan balance back up makes no sense. There has to be a definite benefit to refinancing if you are going to increase debt.

Never get a mortgage with an adjustable interest rate

The main idea when getting a mortgage is to know you will be making the same payment every month at the same interest rate. Even if the rate is lower, don't get tricked into getting an ARM (adjustable rate mortgage). ARM's are commonly used by investors who plan on selling the house much sooner than when their interest rate will adjust.

Never get a mortgage with a balloon option

Having a balloon payment is a big risk, considering things in life constantly change. Only investors should get a balloon payment option when it benefits them. When you have a balloon payment, you are required to pay the loan in full after a determined time period such as 3 year, 5 years, or 10 years. Not everyone will have this amount of money laying around to use to pay off their mortgage. It's a much better idea to pay off your mortgage when it's most convenient to you instead of being forced to pay on a specific date. You will often be offered a lower interest rate when getting a balloon payment option but it's not worth it.

Chapter 15

Reversing the financial tables by using compound interest to your favor

"Compound interest is the most powerful force in the universe."

Albert Einstein

Now that you have paid off your mortgage, let's start making some real magic happen. You should have freed up $2,180 which used to be your mortgage payment, what's next? What should you invest in? Should you simply save or buy another home? The answer is up to you but I will show you one of the most powerful and simplest ways of increasing your capital that requires the least amount of effort. I am not a financial planner, accountant, or attorney (which you should consult with first before considering this option.) so make sure to consult with them first.

Let's use an example of how compound interest can be used.

Let's say you start depositing the same $2,180, which you were paying the bank in mortgage payments, into an interest earning savings account. Since you finished paying off your mortgage 22 years earlier (if you originally had a 30 year mortgage but refinanced to a 15 year mortgage and used the compound savings method and had $500 in rental income as shown in one of the previous chapters), we will calculate how much you could save in those same years which you don't have to make payments on any more.

$2,180 – used to go towards your mortgage payments.

$2,180 – will now go towards an interest earning savings account every month that will allow you to compound interest on an monthly basis (just make sure your bank compounds interest on a monthly basis.).

Let's assume a very modest interest rate of 1%, even though rates can be higher and may fluctuate in those 22 years.

How it can work for you

If you make monthly deposits of $2,180 into a 1% earning savings account that compounds on a monthly basis, you will see your savings grow approximately to:

Year 1: $28,362

Year 2: $54,805

Year 3: $81,513

Year 4: $108,489

Year 5: 135,733

Year 6: $163,250

Year 7: $191,043

Year 8: $219,114

Year 9: $247,465

Year 10: $276,100

Year 11: $305,021

Year 12: $334,231

Year 13: $363,733

Year 14: $393,530

Year 15: $423,626

Year 16: $454,022

Year 17: $484,722

Year 18: $515,729

Year 19: $547,047

Year 20: $578,677

Year 21: $610,624

Year 22: $642,890

What an amazing thing! You have created an enormous amount of money through consistent savings and compound interest.

An initial amount of $2,180 became $642,890 after 22 years.

The results are in

In 22 years, the home you paid off should be worth more than 22 years ago but that's not something you will be guaranteed. The compound savings you have created through persistent and disciplined actions, are something you can count on. The economy can shift up or down but your savings can grow at a consistent rate if you continue making deposits every month.

Don't blame others

Don't depend on others and don't blame others for the financial decisions you make. Talk to your spouse and plan accordingly. Saving and using compound interest in your favor will depend entirely upon you. It will dramatically change your future the sooner you start.

Using both methods of paying off debts and saving through compound interest

Using both methods: 1. Paying off your mortgage in 6-8 years, and 2. Consistently saving the same payments for the remainder of the 22 years to complete a 30 year term, you should have a fully paid off home and a large savings account to retire on and live comfortably off if you keep your expenses low and maintain a reasonable lifestyle. Living within your means will create financial stability and peace of mind throughout the years. Always reserve some money for the things you would like to accomplish in life and for visiting places you have dreamed of going to see.

Putting your hard earned money in high risk investments will not give you predictable future results which, as you age, you will notice become more important to you. This is an example of what you can do in a relatively safe and consistent manner, but the final decision is up to you.

Things you can do to increase the amount of funds you have after 22 years:

1. Shop for the best savings account interest rate.
2. Consider talking to the branch manager as they have the power to give you a slightly higher interest rate.
3. Increase the amount you can deposit every month by renting space in your home.
4. Increase the amount you deposit every month by saving money in other areas such as: lower electrical bills, lower insurance payments, paying off a car or credit card, etc. and using the savings to redeposit into your savings account.
5. Switch to a hybrid or electric car and use the gas savings to deposit in your savings account.

LET'S CONSIDER DIFERENT FUTURE OUTCOMES BASED ON WHAT YOU DO WITH YOUR SAVINGS (assuming the interest is compounded monthly):

If you have a savings account earning 2%

If you have a savings account earning 2% (on average over 22 years) and you deposit the same $2,180 you were paying towards your mortgage every month for 22 years you would accumulate approximately $717,512.

If you have a savings account earning 3%

If you have a savings account earning 3% (on average over 22 years) and you deposit the same $2,180 every month for 22 years you would amass approximately $803,019.

If you make monthly deposits of $2,200 into a savings account earning 1%

If you have a savings account earning 1% (on average over 22 years) and you deposit $20 more than the original $2,180 you would have $2,200 deposited every month for 22 years you would have $648,763.

If you make monthly deposits of $2,500 into a savings account earning 1%

If you have a savings account earning 1% (on average over 22 years) and you deposit $2,500 every month for 22 years you would accumulate approximately $736,861.

If you make monthly deposits of $3,000 into a savings account earning 1%

If you have a savings account earning 1% (on average over 22 years) and you deposit $3,000 every month for 22 years you would amass approximately $883,691.

If you make monthly deposits of $3,000 into a savings account earning 2%

If you have a savings account earning 2% (on average over 22 years) and you deposit $3,000 every month for 22 years you would accumulate approximately $986,134.

If you make monthly deposits of $3,000 into a savings account earning 3%

If you have a savings account earning 3% (on average over 22 years) and you deposit $3,000 every month for 22 years you would have $1,103,501.

SHARE THE KNOWLEDGE

One of the most useful ways to learn what is in this book is by teaching someone else how to pay off their mortgage sooner. What a wonderful thing it would be if more people were out of debt and especially when the debt is large. Mortgages are normally the largest debt most people ever incur in their lifetimes.

Who do you know that owns their home?

Most people who own a home will have a mortgage and will be very interested in learning how they can pay off their mortgage much sooner.

Do you know at least 5-10 people you could share this knowledge with?

Call them and tell them you have valuable information that would benefit them and possibly allow them to retire sooner.

Always remind them to contact their accountant or financial planner for any questions for specific information they may want to ask. For general educational purposes, they will still need what's in this book and you have the power to help another person in need. PAY IT FORWARD.

Information can be very powerful but it is even more powerful when it is shared with others who care.

LEARN - APPLY - SHARE

IMPORTANT VOCABULARY

15 Year Fixed Mortgage Loan: is a loan granted by a bank or lender whose interest rate stays the same for the life of the loan which is a 15 year term and is used to finance the purchase of a real estate property.

30 Year Fixed Mortgage Loan: is a loan granted by a bank or lender whose interest rate stays the same for the life of the loan which is a 30 year term and is used to finance the purchase of a real estate property.

Amortization: is the term used to explain the reduction of the loan balance being paid back in the form of principal payments.

Bi-weekly Payment Plan: is a plan in which mortgage payments are made every two weeks instead of once a month.

Compound Interest: is the term used to explain the addition of interest to the principal sum of a deposit made. It is often referred to as "interest on interest".

Debt: the sum of money owed.

Down payment: the amount a buyer pays to purchase a house in addition to the funds the buyer borrows.

Finance charge: the cost of consumer credit as a dollar amount.

First mortgage: is the term used to describe a security instrument with a first lien position.

Interest rate: when referring to a loan, is the amount charged by the lender and is expressed as a percentage of the principal borrowed.

Loan: money that is borrowed and intended to be paid back with interest.

Loan processor: an individual who performs clerical or support duties as an employee in the processing of a mortgage loan.

Loan-to-value: the relationship between the unpaid principal balance and the appraised value/purchase price (whichever is lower) of the property.

Mortgage: is a loan that a bank or lender grants for the purpose of financing the purchase of a real estate property.

Mortgage loan originator: an individual who takes a mortgage loan application.

Prepayment penalty: a fee paid to the lender (often times, the bank) if the borrower pays off the entire mortgage in a time period sooner than the originally agreed loan maturity.

Principal: when talking about a loan, principal is the amount owed.

This book is dedicated to my father for having motivated me into getting started in the world of mortgages.

www.ingramcontent.com/pod-product-compliance
Lightning Source LLC
Chambersburg PA
CBHW020837210326
41598CB00019B/1934